STRIVE

PRAISE FOR *Strive*

The life we all live is based on the work we put into it. What Tim Hiller provides to us throughout *Strive* is how diligence in pursuing God will always result in a winning lifestyle. Thanks, Tim, for this seed you've sown. I pray it produces much fruit.

GREG JENNINGS
PRO BOWL/ALL PRO NFL WIDE RECEIVER; SUPER BOWL CHAMPION;
FORMER GREEN BAY PACKER, AND CURRENT MIAMI DOLPHIN

Genuine, authentic, and a devoted follower of Jesus Christ . . . those are the first thoughts that come to mind in describing Tim Hiller. These characteristics define his interaction with others, whether he is addressing sports-ministry leaders at a Chaplains Roundtable Conference, on-the-air with Sports Spectrum Radio, or working with young people. Through *Strive*, you will benefit from his approach to the challenges of life, which is rooted in his deep love for Christ and desire for others to know God for themselves.

BILL HOUSTON
LEAD PRODUCER AND CO-HOST OF SPORTS SPECTRUM RADIO

A beautifully written, incredibly positive, addictive guide, packed with valuable insights that will help you on your life journey—one step, one week at a time. I found myself learning and inspired to become a better person with each passing entry.

ADRIAN GOSTICK
NEW YORK TIMES BESTSELLING AUTHOR OF
ALL IN AND *WHAT MOTIVATES ME*

STRIVE

Strive

Life is short.
Pursue What Matters.

Tim Hiller

Published by Deep River Books
Sisters, OR
www.deepriverbooks.com

ISBN: 9781940269634
Library of Congress: 2015944685

Cover design by Jason Enterline

Printed in the USA

CONTENTS

Acknowledgments 11

Foreword by Danny Wuerffel 13

Introduction 15

1. Slide Over 17

2. Dangerous Game 21

3. Classroom of Pain 25

4. Work 29

5. Your Life Is Your Message 33

6. Confident Humility 37

7. Familiar Territory 41

8. First World Problems 45

9. Short Prayer Getaways 49

10. Waiting Rooms 53

11. No Such Thing 57

12. Can They Tell? 61

13. The Pride of Production 65

14. WE > ME 69

15. Closets 73

16. Too Much 77

17. Disguises 81

18. The Cancer of Entitlement 85

19. Focus 89

20. The Danger (and blessing) Of Imitation 95

21. Humbition 99

22. Defining Moments 103

23. Identity Crisis 107

24. Unless 111

25. Keep Saying It 115

26. You Keep What You Give Away 119

27. Pulse Check Friend 123

28. Micromanagement 127
29. What We Can't See 131
30. Family Matters? 135
31. Fake Faith? 139
32. The Noise in Our Heads 143
33. The Exchange 149
34. Stay By Your King 153
35. Always Ambassadors 157
36. The Responsibility of Freedom 161
37. Is This All There Is? 165
38. Shifting His Glance 169
39. Keep Your Tests Tests 173
40. Eye Contact 177
41. Put Your Money Where Your Mouth Is 181
42. Believers? Or Knowers? 185
43. The Call 189
44. Special Friend 193
45. Who Do You Think You Are? 197
46. Parting Words 201
47. Pride in Disguise 205
48. Wasting Time 209
49. How Do You View Him? 213
50. All Work Is Service 217
51. How Thankful? 221
52. Strategic Planning 225
    Notes 229
    About the Author 233

ACKNOWLEDGMENTS

All glory, praise, and honor is due to our great God—the author and perfecter of our faith. His word, the Bible, is the inspiration for each weekly challenge in these pages. I am more and more amazed by who he is and his work in my life each and every day.

It simply would not be possible for you to have this book in your hands without the contribution, support, and input of many amazing people whom God has placed in my life.

First and foremost, to my wife Michelle, the love of my life—thank you. For your support, for helping me find the right words, and for putting up with many, many late nights typing away on my laptop. I love you.

To author Adrian Gostick—thank you for believing in my writing, encouraging me to pursue publishing, and for your candid feedback on the *Strive* manuscript. Your input is woven throughout the book.

To Chad and Joel—thank you for sharing your experiences and learning from publishing your books. Your wise counsel has been incredibly valuable. I am truly grateful.

To the *Strive* editing team: Joel, Josh, Bill, and Danny—thank you is not enough. Your time, effort, and insights made Strive exponentially better. I appreciate your help, but more importantly, I appreciate each of you.

Finally, to Bill Carmichael and the Deep River Books team—thank you for making *Strive* a reality. You are great partners and quality people.

FOREWORD

On August 28, 2005, my wife and I, along with our young son, evacuated the city of New Orleans as Hurricane Katrina was bearing down on our home. Little did we know that everything we owned would soon be under eight feet of water for several weeks.

In the aftermath of the storm, we sat and waited to hear what became of our world: our home, our neighbors, Desire Street Ministries (the inner-city ministry in the Ninth Ward where we worked). The mayor speculated that tens of thousands may have died.

Two days after the storm passed, we saw a picture of our neighbor's house; it had water up to the roof. We realized that everything we owned was gone. But at the same time, while so many people couldn't find their loved ones, there I sat with my wife and son safely beside me.

I had lost everything I had, but I still had everything I needed.

Being a human is tough. It's no simple task discovering what matters, what is important, and what is worth striving for. And even if we feel confident in the goal or destination we want for our journey, it's an entirely different challenge to find the plan and strategy to get there.

In *Strive*, Tim Hiller serves us much like a wise coach, an older brother, a cheerleader, and an encourager. He challenges us to determine what matters in life and gives us engaging, simple, and clear ways to navigate our way.

I have been blessed to know Tim over the last several years, and I'm thankful he's taken the time to give us this book. *Strive* has been an encouragement to me, and I trust it will be for you too.

DANNY WUERFFEL
EXECUTIVE DIRECTOR, DESIRE STREET MINISTRIES
1996 HEISMAN TROPHY WINNER, QUARTERBACK, UNIVERSITY OF FLORIDA

INTRODUCTION

Sanctification—"The life-long process of becoming who God made us to be."

The thing I dislike most about that definition, albeit perfectly accurate, is "life-long." I want to arrive now. I want to fulfill my God-given potential today. I want to become all that God designed me to be this instant.

But I cannot. And neither can you.

In our fast-moving, instant gratification culture, we all want less journey and more destination. But that's not how it works. That is not God's perfect design.

Strive—"To make great efforts to achieve or obtain something."

We all are striving for something every minute of the day, whether we realize it or not. Some of us are striving for more power and status; others for more financial security; to be better parents, spouses, and friends; to advance in our careers; to garner achievement and recognition; or simply to be accepted and loved.

In most cases, these are very noble and understandable pursuits. Our time is short, our lives are busy, and we want these things now. *But do they even matter?* They are temporary and will fade away. Our power and status will disappear, our finances can't leave this world with us, our friends and family will all pass someday, our careers will end, someone will reject us, and eventually, the world will ultimately forget our accomplishments.

But what if we all began striving for the best thing possible—both in this life and the eternal one to come?

Strive is a humble attempt to help us take small steps each week on our journeys to becoming more Christ-like, to making our lives count, to developing into the person who God designed us to be. *Strive* seeks to provide encouragement, challenge, and resources—straight from God's word—to help us live for what really matters. As the Apostle Paul perfectly penned:

"Brothers and sisters, I do not consider myself yet to have taken hold of it. But one thing I do: Forgetting what is behind and straining forward to what is ahead, I press on toward the goal to win the prize for which God has called me heavenward in Christ Jesus." (Philippians 3:13–14)

Let's all *Strive* toward the goal together.

TIM HILLER

[John] did not fail to confess, but confessed freely, "I am not the Messiah." They asked him, "Then who are you? Are you Elijah?" He said, "I am not." "Are you the Prophet?" He answered, "No." Finally they said, "Who are you? Give us an answer to take back to those who sent us. What do you say about yourself?" ...John replied... "Among you stands one you do not know. He is the one who comes after me, the straps of whose sandals I am not worthy to untie."

JOHN 1:20–22, 26–27

DAY 1: NFL rookie mini-camp with the Indianapolis Colts. Welcome to the big leagues, kid.

Rookie mini-camp is three full days of immersion into the team's offensive and defensive systems. The pace is slightly slower because no veteran players are participating in practice. But the competition level is extremely high, and many of the undrafted players are going home at the conclusion of the three days. This is their one and possibly only shot to make a good impression. Only rookies and second-year players participate in rookie mini-camp, and that ended up being a good thing for me.

I entered the quarterback meeting room at the Colts' practice facility. I had always made it my practice in meetings, class lectures, and other learning opportunities to sit in the front of the room. (My wife will tell you this makes me an extreme nerd.) It was the perfect spot to watch film, see the whiteboard, and gather as much information as possible.

Just as I settled in and opened my notebook and binder, I heard a voice come from the back of the room by the door. It was one of the second-year quarterbacks participating in mini-camp.

"That's where Peyton sits."

I did a quick look around, surveyed the situation, made a mental note to never sit in that seat again, and thanked him for the heads up. Clearly not a mistake you want to make day one on the job!

I slid over a chair and began to resettle for the commencement of our meeting.

"That's where he puts his feet."

When you've been NFL MVP five times, been to thirteen Pro Bowls, won a Super Bowl, and also been named Super Bowl MVP, I guess it's safe to say you get two chairs in the meeting room. (Now you see why I'm glad the veterans weren't around!)

Humbled, but also grateful for my teammate's guidance, I slid over again to the other side of the conference table to claim my rightful seat— near the back of the room.

I had some success playing football in college. I had worked unbelievably hard to get to this point. In my own little world, I was number one.

But sometimes, it's our time to slide over.

The longer I live, the more I see that life is a continual process of learning, working hard, rising up, and then being humbled. Sliding over, then sliding over again. And again. Learn, work, rise, be humbled, slide over.

We progress from runny-nosed freshman to high school senior, only to be thrown into the scary new world of college life. We think we know it all as we finish our post-secondary education, only to see how much we don't know in the workplace. We feel good as we get our lives established—until that first child comes along and we realize what a mess we are.

Our health can dissipate in one fragile instant. Wealth can disappear. A loved one we've taken for granted can be gone before we know it. Life is a series of slide-over moments.

How will you handle the next time you have to slide over?

I cannot find a better example of how to handle our slide-over moments than the account of John the Baptist in chapter 1 of the Gospel of John. John is going through this same cycle: he's learning, working hard, and growing in prominence. His ministry is gaining traction, and he's making an impact. He has people's attention, so much so that the religious leaders of the day send their minions to find out who this rising star really is. They're curious.

How will John handle this pivotal moment? By sliding over.

"[John] confessed freely, 'I am not the Messiah'" (v. 20).

John humbly admits his rightful place. He seems to say, "I'm not powerful, I'm not a know-it-all, I'm not even a big success." And then comes the big moment.

John slides over. For Jesus Christ.

"He is the one who comes after me, the straps of whose sandals I am not worthy to untie" (v. 27).

But moreover, in amazing and stunning fashion, John was only paying it forward for Jesus, as the Son of God would soon slide over for someone else God views as very important: you and me.

> Being in very nature God, he did not consider equality with God something to be used to his own advantage; rather, he made himself nothing by taking the very nature of a servant, being made in human likeness. And being found in appearance as a man, he humbled himself by becoming obedient to death—even death on a cross.

PHILIPPIANS 2:6–8

In unbelievable fashion, the King of kings became a slave so that you and I—slaves to our worldly sin—could sit on the throne of Heaven like kings! It's an astonishing reversal and a perfect example of sliding over.

This week, where is God prompting you to slide over? Is there someone at work you can empower to take on more responsibility? Is there someone in your family you need to give a second chance? Do you just need to admit to someone that you were wrong, humble yourself, and apologize?

Let's follow the powerful examples of John and Jesus and slide over for the benefit and service of God and those around us.

THIS WEEK, STRIVE...

- ☐ To pinpoint what is most difficult about sliding over for others. Is it your need for power and control? Is it your pride? Do you fear change?

- ☐ To identify one person in your life that you need to slide over for. Is it your son or daughter? The up-and-comer you're mentoring at work? Someone to whom you owe an apology? Select someone you need to empower by humbling yourself.

- ☐ To find a trusted friend or family member who will hold you responsible to your slide over pledge. Tell them whom you're sliding over for and why you're doing it. Ask them to pray for you and to hold you accountable to your commitment.

Dangerous Game
Week 2

Make a careful exploration of who you are and the work you have been given, and then sink yourself into that. Don't be impressed with yourself. Don't compare yourself with others. Each of you must take responsibility for doing the creative best you can with your own life.

Galatians 6:4–5 (The Message)

When running 26.2 miles on race day, a marathoner's worst enemy is comparison. As the pack of runners bursts through the starting gate and begins the race, every runner's emotions, energy, adrenaline, and nerves are in full force. For months, each runner has been strictly training and setting stringent goals to achieve his or her desired end time.

But the temptation on race day is to look around.

A marathoner's biggest vice is comparing his or her pace to that of the other runners. If anything, the marathoner is better off running the first few miles slower than his or her pace goal, because this strict discipline produces the best chance of a strong finish at the end of the race.

For the marathoner, comparison is a dangerous game. And I've got news for us: We are all marathoners. Life is a marathon. Not a sprint.

I have a confession to make. While running life's marathon, I tend to be a comparison junkie. I tend to look around.

I first had my eyes opened to my tendency to compare when I was competing for the quarterback position at Western Michigan University in 2007. I had suffered a severe knee injury in the final game of 2005 that caused me to miss the entire 2006 season. To say I had been working and waiting for this moment was an understatement!

I relished the chance to compete. It required me to bring my absolute best each and every day. But the biggest struggle through it all was the dangerous game of comparison.

It was an inner battle to not look around each day. A mental melee to not constantly search for an answer to the question, "How am I doing?" Am I watching more film than him? Did I throw the ball better than he did today? Did I complete more passes than everyone else? Am I making better decisions with the football than my competition?

I found myself daily measuring my performance against that of others, rather than measuring my performance against the absolute best I had to give. The issue wasn't just my comparison; it was the yard stick I was measuring against.

But since that quarterback competition in 2007, if I'm brutally honest with you who are reading this, I battle my urge to compare on a daily basis.

As I compose this devotional, I am twenty-eight years old. If I live to be 100, I'm not far removed from completing the first quarter of my time on Earth. But I constantly find myself comparing my first quarter of life to other people's half time or third quarter. I catch myself thinking thoughts like:

- I should be as wise as she is.
- I should have as much money as he does.
- Why am I not in that position yet?
- I have such a long way to go.

The reality is that I shouldn't be comparing my first quarter to anyone else's first quarter. Every life journey is different. None of these thoughts of comparison encourage, edify, or uplift me or anyone around me. They accomplish nothing worthwhile, and they certainly don't honor God. Comparison is a dangerous game.

Don't be like me. Don't compare your beginning to someone else's middle, or your middle to someone else's end. Don't compare the start of your second quarter of life to someone else's third quarter. They are a quarter ahead! It's unrealistic, unhealthy, and unreasonable.

And it isn't trusting God.

The Apostle Paul provides us three simple principles in Galatians 6 to help us defeat the dangerous game of comparison:

1. KNOW YOURSELF

Paul urges us all to study "who you are and the work you have been given, and then sink yourself into that." In other words, defeat comparison by doing your homework. Evaluate who you are—your gifts, your skills, and what you love to do. Examine the work God has given you—your occupation, your family, and your community. Then accept your identity—God has made you just the way you are to impact others right where he's placed you.

I love the way *The Message* paraphrases it—"sink yourself into that." I think of doing a cannon ball into a swimming pool! Jump in, with both feet, into the person God has made you to be!

2. HUMBLE YOURSELF

Paul writes: "Don't be impressed with yourself. Don't compare yourself with others." We can defeat comparison by humbling ourselves. Humility is a peace that accepts one's strengths and limitations. But humility isn't thinking less of yourself. It's thinking of yourself less. A humble person is comfortable in their own skin. That humility and peace allows us to be focused. Because we know who God made us to be, we don't need to compare ourselves with others. We can, instead, focus on maximizing our God-given potential, to become all that God desires us to be in this life.

3. BE YOURSELF

Finally, Paul implores that "Each of you must take responsibility for doing the creative best you can with your own life." God has given you gifts, talents, resources, work to do, people to impact, and the opportunity to grow in him—everything you need to make a difference. There truly is no need to compare! Be who you are! As a pastor of mine wisely put it: "God will never do *for* us what he can do *through* us." We simply must do our best and trust God with the rest!

We each have God-ordained things we must experience—both successes and failures—to become the men and women he is designing us to be. We have wisdom to gain, pain to grow from, and joy to celebrate. We are all works in progress! We are each on a journey that is not our own. It is God's plan, God's path, and God's timing. Contrary to popular belief, we don't set the pace. (One day I will learn this!) God alone is sovereign and in control of our life's marathon.

This week, and in the weeks to come, trust your Heavenly Father as you run your life's race. He knows what is best! Know, humble, and be yourself. "**Don't compare yourself with others,**" rather "**take responsibility for doing the creative best you can with your own life.**"

This week, Strive . . .

- ☐ To identify one area of your life where comparison is a struggle. *Know yourself.* Own your struggle. Is it comparing possessions to what others have? Is it comparing knowledge or experience? Comparing talent or accomplishments? Where do you find yourself falling into comparison?

- ☐ To pinpoint an area of your life where you can put someone else first. Is there a person in your life you need to invest more time in? Is there a new way you can get out and serve others in your community? Remember, *humbling yourself* doesn't mean thinking less of yourself, it means thinking of yourself less!

- ☐ To simply *be yourself* this week by relinquishing control to God. Come before him in prayer and tell him you are giving him your comparison struggle. Simply work hard, do your best, and let God do the rest! Do you feel relief? Comfort? Even joy? How does trusting God help you defeat comparison?

CLASSROOM OF PAIN
WEEK 3

And we know that in all things God works for the good of those who love him, who have been called according to his purpose.

ROMANS 8:28

Pain is not something to fear. Pain is actually a powerful teacher for good.

In August 2000, Super Bowl champion NFL coach Tony Dungy and his wife Lauren adopted a healthy baby boy named Jordan. All seemed well until Jordan received his first set of immunizations—and he didn't cry. Then a few months later he fell off the bed—a normally traumatic experience for a young child. Again he didn't cry. In fact, the more the Dungy's thought about it, Jordan never cried, so they took him to a neurologist for more testing.

Jordan was diagnosed with congenital insensitivity to pain. He is missing a gene in the make-up of his DNA. He feels no pain.

What a great thing! Right?

Think again.

Falls, scars, scrapes, and burns—none of them faze young Jordan. Without the sensation of pain, there is very little Jordan fears.

Psychologists in Europe have conducted research that shows children who are protected from feeling pain actually suffer negative effects as they grow up. Kids who never experience things like scraped knees, bruises, or even broken bones from playing outside and being active actually are far more likely to suffer from intense fears and phobias later in life. Children who never spent time playing on a jungle gym in their childhood years are more likely to be fearful of risks, commitment, and relationships.[1]

We need to be in the classroom of pain sometimes. Pain is a powerful teacher. In the words of Tony Dungy:

Through Jordan, I realized that God allows us to feel pain for a reason: to protect us. God uses many things to show us what to avoid, and painful consequences often teach us lessons quickly. ...Pain prompts us to change behavior that is destructive to ourselves or to others. Pain can be a highly effective instructor.[2]

I can personally testify to the benefit of pain in my life on multiple occasions. The best example took place in 2007. After handing off the football to one of our running backs, I rolled out left to carry out my play action fake. I stepped in a low spot on our practice field and felt an awkward, sharp pain. Adrenaline took over, and I finished practice with no issues.

But the pain kept getting worse.

Fast forward six weeks. After our third game of the season at Missouri, I had to withdraw myself from our Monday night conditioning after practice—something I'd never dream of doing. But the pain was worsening with each step. Something wasn't right.

An x-ray revealed I'd been playing on a broken foot for the past six weeks. Stubborn and unwilling to sit out, I had a metal plate inserted in all my cleats to keep my foot flat while playing. Each day I padded and taped the damaged bone, took large doses of ibuprofen, and gutted it out the rest of the season. I had a screw surgically inserted after our last game.

I've never been as close to the Lord as I was during that stretch of pain. I felt like I was grinding my teeth for four months straight. Every step, every day was painful. It never went away. But I was in prayer constantly. It was the only way I could make it through practice and games, let alone the day. I needed God's strength. I had no choice but to rely on him, every moment and every hour.

Don't miss it in your own life. The classroom of pain can be incredibly useful. Without pain, how would we know what true joy feels like? Without pain, how would we know what is harmful to us? Without pain, how would we be able to handle failure? Without pain, how would we learn to take risks and learn from them? Without pain, how would we be able to appreciate health? Without pain, how could we learn proper boundaries and limits?

Without pain, how can we understand the power of the cross?

Romans 8:28 reminds us that even the worst pain in our lives can ultimately be used by God for good. Paul writes that "in *all things* God works for the good of those who love him." This not only proves true in our lives, we see it in the life of Jesus Christ during his darkest moment: crucifixion. In the words of Pastor Timothy Keller, when Jesus was on the cross, "His body was being destroyed in the worst possible way, but that was a flea bite compared to what was happening to his soul."[3]

His pain for our good.

Whatever pain you're experiencing this week, do two things:

1. ASK THE RIGHT QUESTION.

In the midst of pain, the default question we are tempted to ask is, "Lord, *how* can I get out of this?" We are programmed to escape and avoid pain. Despite the discomfort, realize you're in the classroom of pain for a reason. Instead, let's ask the question, "Lord, *what* do you want me to get out of this?" Don't leave the classroom of pain without gathering wisdom from its instruction.

2. LOOK ON THE CROSS.

The power of the cross lies in the bearer of the pain. The pain meant for us was laid on him. Hell is eternal and apart from Christ is our deserved punishment (see Romans 6:23). But Christ paid that eternal pain in six hours on the cross, fully removing the debt from our shoulders (see John 19:30). Eternity paid for in a day. Imagine the weight of that pain!

This week, consider the lessons to be learned from our pain. Consider the good God has waiting for us when we graduate from pain's classroom. "For our light and momentary troubles are achieving for us an eternal glory that far outweighs them all" (2 Corinthians 4:17).

Consider the magnitude of Christ's pain for us and be grateful. Pain is a powerful teacher for good!

THIS WEEK, STRIVE...

- ☐ To reflect on a painful experience in your life. Was it the loss of a loved one? An illness or injury? Here's the key: What did you learn from it? Are you still learning from it? What do you carry with you from the experience that benefits you to this day?
- ☐ To memorize 2 Corinthians 4:17. Though your painful experience was likely long and incredibly difficult, looking back on it, has the outcome been good? Are you better for it? Would you change anything?
- ☐ To share your painful experience, and the lessons it taught you, with someone else. This may not be easy. It may take time to get to the point where you are ready to do this. Pray and ask for God's guidance about what to share, when to share it, and who to share it with. How can others benefit from your story?

WORK
WEEK 4

*The L*ORD *God took the man and put him in the Garden of Eden to work it and take care of it.*

GENESIS 2:15

Recently, three conversations in which I engaged really had me pondering work and its role in our lives.

One conversation was with a family friend whose teenage son wasn't enjoying his evening and weekend job at a local restaurant. My friend challenged his son to think about something he really wanted, to which the young man replied, "I really want a Ford Mustang." "There you go!" replied my friend. "That's why you're working!" The philosophy was simple—work is a means to an end.

The second conversation was with a sales rep I met with on several occasions. Over time I came to develop a relationship with him and find out he was a Christ follower. We had several meaningful conversations during the course of our business meetings. One was on the topic of work. As I recall it, he joked sarcastically: "Why is it we have to work again? Oh that's right…it's that darn Adam! Thanks Adam!" He was referring to what is known as the fall, man's first sin, recorded in Genesis chapter 3. In verse 17, God tells the first human man, Adam: "Because you listened to your wife and ate fruit from the tree about which I commanded you, 'You must not eat from it,' Cursed is the ground because of you; through painful work you will eat food from it all the days of your life." As before, the philosophy was simple—work is a duty or a punishment.

The third conversation took place with a high school student-athlete. He had been working hard on the practice field but had to wait his turn as older players held down the starting position he was pursuing. However, his interest in sports journalism and a knack for writing earned him statewide recognition for his school work and writing. When I congratulated him, he responded: "Thanks! It's always nice to get recognized for hard work. It makes it all worth it." Once again, the philosophy was simple—work is a pursuit of recognition and accomplishment.

Can this be true? Is work simply a means to an end? Is it simply duty, or even punishment? Is it to garner recognition?

I have to say I disagree with all these viewpoints. I believe God has much more in store for our work and career life.

According to the Centers for Disease Control and Prevention, the average life expectancy in the United States is almost seventy-nine years. That comes out to just over 692,000 hours lived in a lifetime.[1]

On average, Americans work 252 days in a calendar year. Financial analysts typically use 252 when valuing financial investments because it is the number of days markets are open for trading. If an individual works eight hours a day for 252 days, that is just over 2,000 hours of work a year.

If that individual works for forty years before retiring, he or she will have worked 80,640 hours in a lifetime. With a life expectancy of seventy-nine years, on the average, Americans spend about 12 percent of their lives at work.

Now 12 percent seems small, but when factored into a lifetime—that is a little over nine years of a person's life spent at work! This excludes the years we spend earning our education. I don't know about you, but if I am going to dedicate nine years of my life to a cause, it better be well worth it!

According to the Bible, work started with the Creator himself. Work began with God! The first verse of the Bible tells us, "In the beginning, God *created* the Heavens and the Earth." God worked! Throughout Genesis chapter 1, God models an example of how to work hard—with vision, enthusiasm, and a plan for sustained growth. He also models a perfect life rhythm—work six days, rest for one—a model we must be cognizant of in our own lives.

Work for man originated in Genesis 2:15: "The LORD God took the man and put him in the Garden of Eden to *work* it and take care of it."

This simple sentence tells us three powerful things about God's purpose for the work in our lives:

1. ROLE TO FILL

God carefully places each of us in key work roles. God doesn't make mistakes! We may not love all the tasks we do or the pay we receive, but that role is designed to use our God-given skills while preparing and equipping us for even bigger work to come.

2. PLACE TO BE

God has a specific place in which we are to work. For Adam, it was the Garden of Eden. For some it is an office. For others a factory. For others a school. For still others, it is a television studio, or in a vehicle, or at a hospital. Regardless of where we work, that location is God-ordained and a key part of furthering his Kingdom through our impact.

3. RESOURCE TO CARE FOR

God gives us something for which we are to be good stewards. Whatever we do, or wherever we do it, he has entrusted us with something to care for. It could be other people we must look after, a task on the assembly line we must do with excellence, or land we must preserve. It could be finances we need to manage. How we do our work is a direct reflection of our care for God's provision in our life.

Perhaps English Reformer John Ruskin said it best: "The highest reward for a man's toil is not what he gets for it, but what he becomes by it." God has greater plans for our work than paychecks and promotions. Work is part of a greater transformation that is molding us into the men and women designed to be change agents for the Kingdom of God!

THIS WEEK, STRIVE...

☐ To create and complete a to-do list of tasks in your various roles at work, home, school, or anywhere else. As you look over your tasks, pay special attention to the things that don't really excite you. Does God have a lesson to teach you, even in these routine responsibilities? Could you change your heart or attitude to be open to what he might teach you through your work?

☐ To reflect on the various places you've been called to work over the course of your life. Consider where you've gone to school, where you've lived, whom you've met, where you've worked, and what you've done. Where have you felt most useful? Where have you felt most stretched? How has God's hand been present in it all? Thank him for his work in your life along the journey!

☐ To list the top five things God has placed under your care during this season of life. What is on your list? Your family? A group of co-workers? A budget? A product? A department? A team? Put your list somewhere visible as you go through your week. Take a few moments each day to pray that you would care for each thing on the list in a God-honoring way.

YOUR LIFE IS YOUR MESSAGE
WEEK 5

Follow my example, as I follow the example of Christ.

1 CORINTHIANS 11:1

My wife and I recently saw this bumper sticker while out running errands. It featured a quote attributed to Mohandas Gandhi:

> "I like your Christ.
> I do not like your Christians.
> They are so unlike your Christ."

Ouch. If our lives as Christ-followers do not look like Jesus, what do they look like?

A 2011 study by the Barna Group found that "More than three out of four self-identified Christians (78%) strongly agreed that spirituality is very important to them. Yet less than one out of every five self-identified Christians (18%) claims to be totally committed to investing in their own spiritual development."[1] An alarming statistic, to say the least. Meaningful relationships require time and devotion, and a true relationship with Jesus is no different. It appears we want the benefits without the cost. But Gandhi didn't need the Barna Group's data to observe this phenomenon. It was visible to him in daily life.

We are not representing Christ in the world as we should.

Unable to get the bumper sticker's message out of my mind, I did some reading on Gandhi's life and found something interesting. Gandhi's nonviolent movement of civil disobedience didn't just play a key role in India gaining its independence; it thrust him into the spotlight as a well-known global political figure.

In line with his notoriety in both politics and social justice, Gandhi was constantly asked and urged to give a message to the people of the nation who followed him, placing their hope and trust in his leadership. Yet time and again he would decline the opportunity to speak publicly, answering with the response, "My life is my message."

Perhaps Gandhi had once read the words of the Apostle Paul in 1 Corinthians 11:1: "Follow my example, as I follow the example of Christ."

In other words, "Watch me, and do as I do." Consider for a moment what a bold, audacious, and confident statement that is. Consider your life, your relationship with Jesus, your words, and your actions. Would you say that to someone else?

If someone wondered what a Christ-follower's life was supposed to look like, would you be able to say, "Watch me"?

Before you begin to feel intimidated or condemned by this question, please press pause for a moment. We are all flawed human beings. We will fail and make mistakes. We will never reach perfection. Admitting this is the first step toward being a witness for Jesus in our broken society.

But despite our imperfections, we are called to be examples to a watching world. Second Corinthians 5:20 makes this undoubtedly clear: "We are therefore Christ's ambassadors, as though God were making his appeal through us."

Being able to say "Watch me and do as I do" is all about courage to be a model of faith and worthy of following. But it is also the courage to risk failure, to be humble enough to admit a mistake and ask forgiveness.

Being an example to others is a requirement of following Jesus, even though none of us will ever be a perfect example.

So how do we muster the courage to be able to say to a watching world, "Follow my example"? Let's make sure we don't miss the end of Paul's statement: "Follow my example, *as I follow the example of Christ.*"

Paul wasn't saying, "Follow Paul." He was saying, "Watch Paul follow Jesus." His focus wasn't on being perfect. His focus was on being in relationship with the one who is perfect—Jesus Christ, the son of God.

Given that 78 percent of "Christians" say their faith is important, but only 18 percent of them are committed to their personal spiritual development, I'd say that being in relationship with Jesus is a great place for all of us to start.

If we want to make an impact and change the world around us, we need to dwell on Jesus. We must study the man's life. We need to read how he lived, what he did, and the things he said. We should consider their implications on our own lives. And then we must follow his example. As we work, serve, speak, make decisions, manage our money, and raise our kids, "Follow the example of Christ."

Only then can we say, "Follow my example" because we're walking in the footsteps of the One who first walked the path. Lead others by following Jesus.

He may not have been a Christ follower, and I know he wasn't perfect, but Gandhi is right. Our life is our message, and we only get one life and one chance to send the message.

Today, remember your life is your message. People are watching. What message are you sending?

THIS WEEK, STRIVE....

- ☐ To spend time crafting the message you want your life to send. You should be able to capture it in three sentences or less. Whom or what do you want to impact? How are you going to do it? Why are you doing it? Can others decipher your message from observing your life? Does anything need to change?

- ☐ To read the Gospel of John in its entirety. That's just three chapters each day for seven days. What were some of the key life messages Jesus exemplified? How did he live them out before a watching world? What did you notice? What did you learn?

- ☐ To identify one quality of Jesus you will seek to better exemplify in your own life. Is it love? Service? Sacrifice? How will you point others to Christ through the way in which you live?

CONFIDENT HUMILITY
WEEK 6

So do not throw away your confidence; it will be richly rewarded. You need to persevere so that when you have done the will of God, you will receive what he has promised.

HEBREWS 10:35–36

I was a junior playing varsity high school basketball, and things were going very well. Except at the free-throw line. They call it the "charity stripe" for a reason. Free points. Uncontested opportunities to score. But my percentage that year had dwindled below 60 percent.

In an effort to stir me from my shooting slumber, a teammate's family member offered some advice. Every time I was fouled and had the opportunity to go to "the stripe," I was to say in my head: "I'm the man. This is why I'm here."

I'm not proud of the fact that this self-centered phrase became my free-throw mantra. From then on, I mentally recited that line every time I dribbled the ball in preparation to shoot a free throw. It gave me the certainty, albeit false, that I couldn't miss. But it also filled my head with arrogant thoughts that I was better than I truly was. Was this the right approach?

My free-throw experience is an example of something we all have experienced at some point in life. Anytime we pursue success, there are two equal and opposite forces at work: certainty and arrogance.

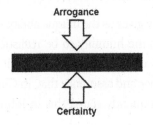

The certainty of being sure that our desire for success will happen. The arrogance that we think we know best—that we are better, smarter, or more important than we really are.

There is clearly a delicate balance in play here. A line of equilibrium we must toe but not cross. We must be certain in order to succeed in our endeavors. But we mustn't overstep from certainty into arrogance.

How do we live with the certainty of faith, but yet remain humble as God desires?

Thankfully, God's word has defined this line for us. Confident humility.

Hebrews 10:19 tells us "we have confidence...by the blood of Jesus." It is not so much about whether we are confident, it's about the object of our confidence. And God strongly reminds us in his word that the object of our confidence is to be him.

Not our abilities, bank accounts, prior accomplishments, or our connections. Our confidence is to stem directly from Christ.

Hebrews 10:35–36 tells us that this Christ-centered confidence "will be richly rewarded" and that it will give us the unique ability to do three things:

1. PERSEVERE THROUGH ADVERSITY ("YOU NEED TO PERSEVERE...")

Confident humility gives us the unique ability to overcome challenges. It gives us the humility to be realistic and realize that things are not always going to go well. But it also gives us the powerful confidence and assurance that, in Christ, we will overcome. Jesus so eloquently stated this in John 16:33—"In this world you will have trouble (*humility*). But take heart! I have overcome the world" (*confidence*).

2. TRUST IN GOD'S PLAN ("SO THAT WHEN YOU HAVE DONE THE WILL OF GOD...")

Confident humility gives us the unique ability to trust an unknown future to a known God. This requires surrendering (*humility*) our goals and dreams to the Lord, and boldly trusting (*confidence*) that what he has in store for us is best. This is only truly fulfilled in the power of Christ.

3. FIND TRUE SUCCESS, IN GOD'S EYES ("YOU WILL RECEIVE WHAT HE HAS PROMISED.")

Confident humility gives us the unique ability to redefine success—and to align it with God's heart. We must admit (*humility*) we've been pursuing worldly pursuits, and place our hope in the success God offers—eternity with him (*confidence*).

Today, work hard and pursue your goals. But do so with confident humility—rooted in Christ Jesus—the One who gives us the ability to persevere, trust, and find true success for his glory.

THIS WEEK, STRIVE...

- ☐ To memorize Hebrews 10:35-36. Read it five times each day this week. What challenge is God asking you to remain confident in the midst of?
- ☐ To make a list of three things that you are placing your confidence in other than God. Look at the list each day this week. Pray for God's help to not depend on these worldly things. Then, at the end of this week, tear up the list and throw it away! You're getting a fresh start by placing your confidence in him alone!
- ☐ To write a personal definition of success. Does it align with God's definition? Do you need to do any redefining?

FAMILIAR TERRITORY
WEEK 7

They said to Moses, "Was it because there were no graves in Egypt that you brought us to the desert to die? What have you done to us by bringing us out of Egypt? Didn't we say to you in Egypt, 'Leave us alone; let us serve the Egyptians'? It would have been better for us to serve the Egyptians than to die in the desert!"

EXODUS 14: 11–12

The Israelites said to them, "If only we had died by the LORD's hand in Egypt! There we sat around pots of meat and ate all the food we wanted, but you have brought us out into this desert to starve this entire assembly to death."

EXODUS 16:3

One of the most difficult challenges of my collegiate football career was altering my throwing motion. Throughout high school, and even before that, I had thrown the ball *my way*. Daily practice had made my throwing motion second nature. It was engrained in my muscle memory. And after years and years of hard work, practice, and repetition, I'd gotten pretty good at throwing my way.

But good is the enemy of great. And great is the enemy of best.

When I got to college, my coaches saw hidden potential that could be tapped with a few mechanical alterations to my throwing motion. I could put more power behind the throw and spin the ball with more revolutions. There was more accuracy to be had.

The process was terribly frustrating. At first, the new motion felt horribly awkward. Sometimes the ball came out perfectly. Sometimes it wobbled and lacked power. I sometimes unknowingly reverted back to my old throwing habits. It was a constant struggle to make the new motion second nature.

The biggest battle I fought was going back to what was familiar.

Slipping back into familiar territory doesn't just apply to quarterbacks changing their throwing technique. It happens to all of us in our daily lives.

We know God is asking us to change some aspect of our life. We know it is necessary to grow in relationship with him. But we don't want to put in the hard work to change.

Or worse, we just don't want to change. We are comfortable where we are. It could be a bad relationship. We know we should get out, but staying put is simpler and more comfortable. It could be a dishonest habit. We should change, but continuing the habit is easier and much less work. Maybe God is calling us to step out in faith and serve him. We should do it, but saying no is more convenient.

Familiar territory.

Even though we could have what is best by putting in some effort, we settle for what is good because it is easy and safe.

In this week's Scripture, we see two examples of this desire to return to familiar territory. God's people, the Israelites, have been enslaved in Egypt for hundreds of years. As a result, they have grown fully accustomed to Egyptian culture—observing their holidays, worshipping their gods, and eating their food. But under the leadership of Moses, the Israelites are led out of bondage on a journey to the Promised Land God set apart for them.

In the first example, we find the Israelites at the edge of the sea with the Egyptian army bearing down on them. No place to go. In their fear of the unknown, they desperately cry to return to what is familiar—Egypt—saying, "It would have been better to serve the Egyptians than to die in the desert!" (Exodus 14:12).

In the second example, we find the Israelites complaining that they are hungry. "If only we had died by the LORD's hand in Egypt!" the angry mob cries. "There we sat around pots of meat and ate all the food we wanted!" (16:3).

Comfort over uncertainty. Easy over hard. Convenience over challenge. Slipping back into familiar territory.

Yet in these examples, we also see God's provision and faithfulness everywhere. In the first, God parts the sea, allowing the Israelites to escape the pursuing Egyptians. In the second, God supplies a bread-like substance called manna to provide for their hunger. And even in the case of a struggling quarterback, God was a constant companion—giving patience to endure the difficult days and building hope with each small victory of a well-thrown ball.

In some form, we can all draw hope from these stories in this: if we commit to escaping familiar territory, if we step out in faith and stick to the plan God has set before us, even when it is uncomfortable, he will provide. He will be faithful, and we will be changed for the better.

Step out in faith today! Make the changes God is asking you to make. He has your best interests in mind because he loves you. Let's not settle for familiar territory.

THIS WEEK, STRIVE...

☐ To make a list of everything that is comfortable and familiar in your life. Maybe it's your home and possessions. Maybe it's your friendships and relationships. Maybe it's a habit or a daily routine. List as many things as you can.

☐ To select at least one thing on your comfort list that is holding you back. Maybe your rigid routine is keeping you from meeting new people you could impact. Maybe your possessions are keeping you from giving generously to God's work in the world. Circle one thing that is hindering growth.

☐ To list three steps you will take to change the familiar comfort you circled. Please spend time in prayer, seeking God's will for what you will change. How will you shake things up? What might God be calling you to change? What will you consider trying? Who could you ask to hold you accountable?

FIRST WORLD PROBLEMS
WEEK 8

There was a rich man who was dressed in purple and fine linen and lived in luxury every day. At his gate was laid a beggar named Lazarus, covered with sores and longing to eat what fell from the rich man's table. Even the dogs came and licked his sores. The time came when the beggar died and the angels carried him to Abraham's side. The rich man also died and was buried. In Hades, where he was in torment, he looked up and saw Abraham far away, with Lazarus by his side. So he called to him, "Father Abraham, have pity on me and send Lazarus to dip the tip of his finger in water and cool my tongue, because I am in agony in this fire." But Abraham replied, "Son, remember that in your lifetime you received your good things, while Lazarus received bad things, but now he is comforted here and you are in agony."

LUKE 16:19–25

I had a really frustrating day at the end of last week. You know the type—a day where each passing hour seems to only beg the question, "What's going to go wrong next?"

The budget meeting I was asked to host to start the morning didn't go so well. As a result, I needed to have a couple difficult discussions with colleagues that their roles at work were going to change. This led to a not-so-fun reprimanding from another co-worker. And it wasn't even lunch time yet!

As I stole away to enjoy a few moments of quiet while I ate lunch, I opened my laptop to catch up on some things. Sipping my red Gatorade, my eyes widened as I found 172 unread messages in my e-mail inbox. Just as I went to read the first message (about the lovely budget meeting!), out of the corner of my eye I noticed a small red puddle on my desk where my Gatorade bottle had been sitting. I glanced down at my lap. Sure enough, there was a small leak in the bottle. Red polka-dot khaki pants for the rest of the day!

After a fairly uneventful afternoon I headed home, glad the day was finally through. As I sat in traffic awaiting the vehicle in front of me to make a left turn, I noticed a car approaching behind me at a high rate of speed. And it wasn't slowing down. At all. The collision into my bumper felt a lot like jolting up in bed from a nightmare. Only, despite my wishes, I wasn't dreaming.

After two hours with police, insurance agents, and body shop workers, I was ready to forget this day. When I got home, I went upstairs to take a hot shower. I should've anticipated it by then, but for some odd reason I was caught off guard. The water never warmed up. Hot water heaters are not cheap to replace.

Let's just say, it wasn't really my day!

Fortunately I haven't had too many days like that since. But when life throws me some "mayhem," like Allstate Insurance depicts in their commercials, I've been trying something new: a problem inventory.

Maybe you'll find this exercise useful too. Review each problem you faced throughout the day. Then flip it on its head. *Find the blessing in it.*

So my budget meeting, my discussions with colleagues, and my friendly meeting with a co-worker didn't go so well? *I'm fortunate to have a job.* (36 percent of people in Afghanistan don't.)

So my e-mail inbox is bursting at the seams? *I'm fortunate to have Internet access.* (About 65 percent of the world doesn't.)

So I spilled something on my pants? *I have clothes to wear and food to eat.* (900 million people in the world are hungry.)

So I had a fender bender? *I'm blessed to own a car.* (Only about 10 percent of people in the world own one.)

So I didn't have hot water for my shower? *I'm lucky to have clean water.* (780 million people lack access to clean water.)

So how bad is my day sounding now?

The term *first-world problems* (FWPs) has become a tongue-in-cheek phrase that refers to the frustrations, complaints, and trivial inconveniences of people living in first-world countries. But consider the concept of FWPs more seriously for a moment.

They're most of what we deal with *every day*. In the United States, the majority of issues you and I face are FWPs. There are certainly exceptions to the rule. Hunger, poverty, and illness still abound in our nation. But the reality is that most of us take for granted our easy access to clean water, public transportation, and quality medical care. Rather, we find ourselves concerned about trivial things like how our lawn looks, how many people liked our last Facebook post, if our curtains match, answering our e-mail, and what other people think of us. First-world problems.

One of the things I've grown very passionate about is a ministry in the community where I live that takes FWPs and blows them to smithereens. I'm blessed to serve on its advisory board, and I can tell you— the model has tremendous potential to invoke cultural change in teenagers.

The ministry's leadership team takes inner-city high school students, whom society is *falsely* telling, "You don't have much going for you," and trains them for a year in African culture. During the year of training, the teens participate in many service projects and team-building activities to prepare for the big moment—a two-week service trip to Sierra Leone, where the students see what it really means to "not have much going for you."

In the words of Oliver Wendell Holmes Jr., "A mind that is stretched by a new experience can never go back to its old dimensions."

Maybe we all need that.

Before you go to Delta.com and start searching for flights to Freetown, Sierra Leone, hear me out. If you have the chance to serve others abroad, go do it. But perspective change is possible in the next five to ten minutes, right here, right now.

And it comes from this week's chilling Scripture from Luke 16. Consider two questions:

1. WHEN DO YOU WANT GOOD THINGS?

"Son, remember that in your lifetime you received your good things, while Lazarus received bad things, but now he is comforted here and you are in agony." Do you want "good things" now for about eighty years, or do you want them for all eternity? When we consider the fate of the rich man in Luke 16, it's a harsh reminder that the FWPs we deal with each day are often trivial and temporary.

2. WHO HAS A NAME?

Note who has a name in this week's Scripture passage. The rich man is referred to as "the rich man." He has no name! But the poor man is called Lazarus. The poor man has a name! We may have a name in our community, business, and sphere of influence, but the poor have a name in the eyes of God. And those holy eyes are the only ones that matter. Are you serving and helping those who have problems far greater than your FWPs?

This week, you will confront first-world problems frequently. At the end of each day, I challenge you to conduct a problem inventory and to count your many blessings. Then pick a blessing and give it away. Let's store up "treasures in heaven" (Matthew 6: 20) as we serve those in need all around us.

THIS WEEK, STRIVE...

- ☐ To take a surplus inventory. Literally walk through your home, search your car, look at what you have and list everything that you don't really need. How long is your list?
- ☐ To review the surplus list you compiled. I challenge you to give away, no strings attached, three things on your list. Monitor how difficult it is to let go of your possessions. What was difficult about selecting what to give away?
- ☐ To reflect on your surplus experiment. How did it feel to give away three things that you didn't need? Did it help someone else meet his or her needs? Out of our excess, we can meet the legitimate needs of others. Pray and ask for God to reveal more ways you can use your surplus to meet the needs of those who are suffering.

SHORT PRAYER GETAWAYS
WEEK 9

But when he saw the wind, he was afraid and, beginning to sink, cried out, "Lord, save me!"

MATTHEW 14:30

I hate it when I get a knot in my shoelaces.

A vice-grip knot developed as I tried to untie my shoes the other day. It was tied tighter than a group hug in a phone booth. I tweaked, yanked, twisted, reconfigured—I even took a chunk out of my fingernail picking at the deadly knot. I got angry. I ripped off my shoe, put it by the breezeway door, and got away from the situation.

Guess what I had to do the next morning?

Put my shoes on. The knot was still there.

"Great," I thought.

But within 90 seconds I had the lethal knot untied.

What happened?

I got away. And when I came back to the problem, things were better. The problem was still there. It hadn't changed at all. But I did.

I had been tired from a long day, stressed out about some things. I had a lot on my mind. I was impatient and growing more and more angry by the second from the industrial-strength knot in my shoelace.

I needed to change. And when I got away from the situation, I did change.

Once in a while, we need a chance to renew our attitude, an opportunity to clear the mind and find a fresh outlook. We need to regain our perspective that not everything revolves around us and the problem at hand is not the end of the world.

Sometimes we just need a getaway. And we can take one anytime. At the feet of Jesus.

Any time of day, any place, any situation . . .we have the opportunity to get away and come back changed. Think mini-Caribbean cruise.

Through prayer.

As far as I can tell, the end of Matthew 14:30 is the shortest prayer in the entire Bible: "Lord, save me!" I just prayed that out loud and timed myself on my watch. It took me 1.51 seconds to pray that prayer.

Someone said to me last week—and sadly I've said this myself many times too—"It's hard for me to find time to pray."

Are you kidding me? Don't try that excuse. You have 1.51 seconds to spare. Pray short prayers.

Pray longer prayers, of course. Spend long periods of focused, uninterrupted, undistracted time with the Lord—in prayer and in his word—whenever you are able. Please do that. You must. Jesus did it all the time! (See Mark 1:35 and Luke 6:12 for just two examples.)

But this requires quiet, solitude, peace, and focus. And a lot of life is fast-paced, chaotic, wild, and crazy. Are you going to stop praying when your second child is born? Are you going to stop spending time with God because you have a big project due in forty-eight hours at work? Are you going to ignore your Heavenly Father because you have too much going on?

What are you going to do? Pray short prayers.

"Lord, save me."

"God, use me."

"Jesus, guide me."

"Lord, give me words." (This one takes 1.93 seconds!)

"Father, help me serve."

"God, grant me wisdom."

"Lord, forgive me."

Do the problems go away? Sometimes. Do they change? Occasionally. Do you? *Yes.*

And that's all the difference. It's the difference needed to be a difference maker for Jesus.

Today, take a few 1.51-to-1.93-second getaways to be with Jesus.

Pray early. Pray often. And when necessary, pray short prayers!

THIS WEEK, STRIVE...

- ☐ To write down seven short prayers you need to pray frequently. Capture them on paper and put them where you will see them often.
- ☐ To pray each of your seven short prayers this week. Focus on praying one throughout the day each day—while you are in the car, while you are walking around your workplace, while you're going about your day.
- ☐ To reflect on your week of focused prayer. How did your short prayer getaways change you? How did they help you approach the challenges and the highlights of the week? How did God equip you for the things you faced?

WAITING ROOMS
WEEK 10

I remain confident of this: I will see the goodness of the LORD in the land of the living. Wait for the LORD; be strong and take heart and wait for the LORD.

PSALM 27:13–14

On December 14, 2008, I was sitting at the desk in my bedroom in the townhouse where I lived with three of my college teammates, studying for a final exam and preparing for our bowl game just two weeks away.

In the background, my laptop was logged on to a local radio station that carried Western Michigan University's women's basketball games over the Internet. Michelle, my then-girlfriend and now wife, was a member of the team. They were on the road in Des Moines, Iowa, playing Drake University.

The game was close. I set aside my textbook and scouting reports. Michelle had come off the bench to score some points. The announcer's voice grew louder as one of the guards got a steal and threw the ball ahead to Michelle on a fast break for a lay-up.

Then I heard Michelle yelling in pain.

An opposing player had undercut her as she laid the ball in. As Michelle came to the ground, her body rotating from the contact, her left foot landed—and didn't rotate. Her ACL and MCL gave way, resulting in major damage to her meniscus and articular cartilage.

Since that fateful day, Michelle has undergone thirteen (yes, thirteen) surgeries to try and repair the damage to her knee. We have spent many days in hospitals, surgery centers, doctor's offices, and waiting rooms. And along the way, the Lord has revealed an area of our lives where we are unfinished works in progress: waiting.

Michelle and I are "get-it-done" people. When we need an answer, we want it now. If we need to buy something, we go get it right away. If we need to talk to someone, they better pick up the phone. If something needs to be done, we want it completed yesterday.

But God is teaching us how to wait well.

Just a hunch, but I bet you hate waiting too. Our world is an enabler. Our world has enabled us to be impatient. And our world has a word for our impatience: *Good*.

The world says it's good to have e-mail responses at my fingertips anytime I want via my tablet or laptop. The world says it's good to have television channels devoted to world news twenty-four hours a day, seven days a week. The world says it's good to have apps on my phone that allow me to shop, define words, hold a meeting, post my social status, and compose presentations all in a matter of minutes.

Or is it?

Perhaps we're being trained in impatience every single day. Patience has moved from being a virtue to being disdained. Impatience has moved from being scorned to being celebrated. This is the new standard operating procedure of our twenty-first-century world.

I've got news for all of us: God doesn't operate like our world does.

Sometimes in this life, we will have to wait. But please don't miss this; it's a powerful lesson the Lord has taught me over the last several years:

What we do while we wait may be more important than what we are waiting for.

During this waiting season, I took time to read Jeff Manion's stellar book, *The Land Between: Finding God in Difficult Transitions*. Manion uses Israel's exodus journey through the Sinai Desert—"the land between" their former home in Egypt and their future home in the Promised Land—as a metaphor for the difficult transitions we face in life. The land between represents what we all dread: waiting.

Manion describes the dichotomy we face when we wait. It is "fertile ground for complaint and emotional meltdown" he writes, but also "fertile ground for God's provision, God's discipline, and for faith to grow."[1] The choice is ours.

Waiting matters. Waiting is an opportunity.

So what are some practical tips for the waiting in our lives? In this week's Scripture text, the Psalmist offers us three:

1. REMAIN CONFIDENT.

Confident of what? Confidence that "I will see the goodness of the LORD" the Psalmist writes. Confident that God is at work while I wait and that my faith in him will remain firmly rooted and unshakeable.

2. BE STRONG.

Waiting is tough. There's no silver bullet or magic pill. There's no iPhone or Android app to time warp ahead. We must go to God early and often to draw strength and purpose from our waiting.

3. TAKE HEART.

In other words, be encouraged! Have hope! God has great plans on the horizon! Jesus has overcome the greatest foes—sin and death—so with him I will overcome this time of waiting.

Confidence, strength, and heart will allow us to wait well. But we still must wait. Rather than asking, How do I get out of this? we must ask, God, what do you want me to get out of this?

This week, whatever you are waiting on, wait well! And may God use your waiting to mold you into the person he designed you to be—a man or woman well equipped to serve and honor him!

THIS WEEK, STRIVE...

☐ To identify the things that create the most impatience in your life. What causes you to anxiously rush? Is it technology constantly at your fingertips? Is it your packed calendar and busy schedule? Why do you find yourself struggling to wait?

☐ To monitor what you tend to do while you wait. Are you able to be still? Do you pray? Or are you restless? Must you constantly seek out things to do? Are your waiting tendencies healthy or harmful?

☐ To memorize Psalm 27:14. How might God mold, shape, and change you for the better the next time you face a period of waiting?

No Such Thing
Week 11

For in him all things were created: things in heaven and on earth, visible and invisible, whether thrones or powers or rulers or authorities; all things have been created through him and for him. He is before all things, and in him all things hold together.

COLOSSIANS 1:16–17

One of the difficult parts of preparing to play professional football was the agent selection process.

After my junior season of college football, it seemed like there were at least two phone calls a week from prospective sports representation firms, in addition to the piles and piles of promotional literature that came in the mail. Each interaction told of the glitz and glamour of selecting that firm. It was like the collegiate recruiting process all over again.

After evaluating the options, my family and I prayerfully narrowed the long list down to five firms to meet with. While I remember all the meetings well, one in particular stands out in my mind.

One of the agent suitors was a young man who was just starting his career in one of the prospective firms. He had a presentation for us about his journey to his current point as a sports agent.

He had clearly paid his dues. He'd done grunt work. He'd moved all over the country. He'd been an intern for years. He'd worked for free. He'd bought his time and waited patiently. He'd waited and worked for this moment.

And he was proud of it. At the bottom of his résumé slide, below these many "wait your turn" career stops, were three words: "Self-Made Man."

That day, we eliminated the "self-made man" from contention to be my NFL agent. Why? Three more words: no such thing.

It's an incredibly humbling pill to swallow when we truly think about "our" so-called accomplishments. When we truly, openly, and honestly consider the things "we've done" in our lives, we come to a stark realization: We've "accomplished" very little.

Consider your journey. The person you "coincidentally" met at just the right time, that led to a relationship that turned into an opportunity. The phone call that "just happened" to come on the perfect day and opened a door you never saw. The "inadvertent" change of plans that ended up being the best thing that ever happened to you. The "accidental" discovery that put you on a whole new path.

Do you really think you "accomplished" the things that led you to where you are today? It's hard to admit, but if we're brutally honest with ourselves, we see that God is more responsible for the accomplishments of our lives than we are.

These "coincidental" meetings, "just happened" phone calls, "inadvertent" changes, and "accidental" discoveries were all perfectly God ordained. They didn't happen by chance. We are all given abilities, time, opportunities, resources, and people—all placed into our lives at exactly the right moment.

God's moment. They are his possession.

These perfect provisions are all a wonderful gift from our Heavenly Father. And when we see him face-to-face one day, we will be required to give an account of how we used all with which he has entrusted us.

There is no self-made man or woman. There is no such thing.

Sometime very soon, someone is going to give you credit for something you've "accomplished." It will be tempting to accept all the acclaim—but you know better. We are all the sum of others' investments in us, God's gifts to us, and his perfect grace—holding it all together. Take the recognition and pass it on. Give it away, knowing that "all things have been created through him and for him."

THIS WEEK, STRIVE...

☐ To name the one accomplishment or thing you are most proud of in your life. Is it your family? An award? A project or position?

Select one source of personal pride.

☐ To write down everything associated with your accomplishment or pride point that was outside of your control. Could be someone giving you the opportunity. Could be help that you received. Could be a circumstance that changed in your favor. List everything you can think of that you had no control over.

☐ To spend time in prayer, thanking God for his role in allowing your accomplishment or pride point to occur. Look at all the many things that fell into place but had little to do with you. Praise him that he has a perfect and all-knowing plan for our lives!

CAN THEY TELL?
WEEK 12

When they saw the courage of Peter and John and realized that they were unschooled, ordinary men, they were astonished and they took note that these men had been with Jesus.

ACTS 4:13

A good friend of mine recently received a wake-up call.

His company conducted internal corporate culture surveys to gather information on employees' satisfaction with their work, their departmental leadership, and the overall environment around the office. As the head of his department, he provided feedback to his superiors, but he also received feedback about his leadership from all his direct reports.

My friend was very interested in the results, but he wasn't concerned about the survey at all. His department had been out-performing expectations. Revenue and volume were way up. His team was posting exceptional growth numbers. Everyone was working hard. Everyone seemed to be meshing well as a team. Morale and engagement appeared very high.

As expected, in many categories, the team's results were stellar. The team was excited about their work and enjoyed collaborating together each day. My friend received high marks from the team about his leadership and managerial skills. Everyone felt they were doing meaningful work that made a difference.

But one portion of the results caught him off guard. One of the qualities his direct reports had to rate was: "My manager cares about me as a person."

It was his lowest score.

Consider your day yesterday. Reflect on those you spoke with and how you interacted with them. Ponder where your focus rested. Was it solely on your work and being productive? Or was it on people and investing yourself into their lives? Look back on your actions—what you did and how you went about it. What did you spend your time on? How did you treat others? Think about how you handled the interruptions or problems that came your way. What did you do? How did you react?

After replaying your day, what if I were to tell you that a poll was taken of the ten people who were around you most throughout the day, and the simple question they were asked was:

"Does (*your name here*) care about me as a person?"

How would you score?

I've often heard the old adage thrown around: "Character is who you are when no one is watching." And to a certain extent this is true. But the reality is, people can only see our character when they are watching us. We may care about someone as a person in our heart and mind, but if no one can see external evidence of our concern, can they tell we care?

External actions are evidence of internal beliefs. Our deeds are what show our creeds.

What do your actions say you believe?

In one of the most grandiose moments of their ministry, chronicled in the book of Acts, Peter and John are questioned by the cynical religious leaders of the Sanhedrin. Others have taken notice of their actions and words leading up to this point. They've just healed a crippled man. They've been boldly proclaiming the Gospel of Christ. And now they are before the religious "cream of the crop"—the teachers of the law, the intellectual elite of the day, the Ivy League of theology. And though Peter and John were "ordinary men" who "were unschooled," something incredible happens.

This group of the religious elite had been listening to Peter's and John's words, watching their actions, studying their demeanor, and scrutinizing their every move. And they came to an astonishing conclusion.

The religious leaders "took note that these men had been with Jesus."

By simply watching and listening, can others say the same of you? Can they tell? Are your actions indicative of your personal relationship with Jesus? Or are you too busy "moving the needle" at work to care?

Are your words filled with grace, love, and thoughtfulness? Or are you too concerned with being productive to show Christ-like love in conversation? Are you seeking opportunities to serve and put others before yourself? Or are you only thinking about what's in it for you?

Do your daily words and deeds say to a watching world, "I know Jesus"? Or do they say something else?

Perhaps like my friend, you need a good wake-up call today. Has the pressure to produce and perform has gotten the best of you? Maybe your busy schedule has distracted you from slowing down, looking around, and seeing the opportunities for impact. Remember that your words and deeds are always on display to a watching world—a hurting and broken world—a world in need of a Savior. And the person to present that Savior to someone in need just might be you!

This week, step back and honestly ask yourself, Do others know I'm in relationship with Jesus? Can they tell? Let's take to heart the difference we can make in others' lives—every day and every hour. The display of our words and deeds might be the only Bible someone ever reads and the only church someone ever visits! Let's make sure they can tell that we've been with Jesus!

THIS WEEK, STRIVE...

- ☐ To perform a calendar evaluation. Look over your week this week. Does looking at how you'll spend your time in the days ahead show that you know Jesus? Does something need to change? *Can others tell?*
- ☐ To perform a budget evaluation. Look at where your money went over the last few weeks. Does looking at your bank transaction register or credit card statement show that you know Jesus? Does something need to change? *Can others tell?*
- ☐ To perform a behavior evaluation. Attempt to assess your words and actions, how you speak to and treat others. Does your behavior show that you know Jesus? Does something need to change? *Can others tell?*

THE PRIDE OF PRODUCTION
WEEK 13

You may say to yourself, "My power and the strength of my hands have produced this wealth for me." But remember the LORD your God, for it is he who gives you the ability to produce wealth, and so confirms his covenant, which he swore to your ancestors, as it is today.

DEUTERONOMY 8:17–18

There's a football that sits on a shelf in my basement. It's embossed with a Western Michigan University Bronco logo and the following statement: "99 Career Touchdown Passes."

And while it serves as a reminder of a special memory, it also reminds me of the ugliness of pride that can lurk in our human hearts.

It was October 2009. The Central Michigan game. A storied rivalry for the Western Michigan University football program. We were hosting our nemesis from up north at home in front of a great crowd.

Late in the first half, coming out of a time-out, we found ourselves driving for a needed touchdown, but in a third and long situation, expecting their defense to sit back and play coverage, we had a good play call ready as we took the field.

However, as I progressed through the cadence, it became obvious the defense had a blitz dialed up as they rotated into a man-to-man scheme. Seeing their weaker safety approaching to match up on one of our best playmakers, I changed the pass protection and the route combination to give him a chance to make a play on a slower defender. We would either score or be forced to face fourth down.

I held the ball long enough to let our receiver get some separation from the defender while I kept the free safety in the middle of the field with my eyes. I released the ball with some air under it as I took a shot in the chest from one of the blitzing linebackers. I didn't see what happened until I heard the crowd and saw the very end of the play.

Touchdown!

What made this moment a little different from other touchdown moments was that this one broke the existing school record for career touchdown passes, which had stood for about a decade. In addition, the previous record holder was my former quarterback coach, a mentor, and a good friend.

As I met my teammates in the end zone and headed back to the sideline, I caught a glimpse of a special message on the scoreboard paying tribute to the record. After speaking on the sideline phones with the coaches up in the press box and grabbing a drink, I took a seat on the bench.

For a couple minutes, I found myself pridefully basking in the glory of this special moment.

"I set this record."

But who protected me and kept me off my back to deliver the ball? The offensive line. And who, time and again, made great plays on the receiving end of the football? Our wide receivers and tight ends. And who put our offense in a position to succeed with great play calling? Our coaching staff. And, at the core of it all, how was any of this possible?

"Remember the LORD your God, for it is he who gives you the ability to produce."

I had to shake myself quickly from my ugly, prideful state. Yes, this was a special moment, but I was taking credit and claiming praise for something that, ultimately, had little to do with me.

We do this all the time, do we not? The pride of production.

Think about the credit we pridefully claim on a daily basis, even with the simplest things. Credit that was never rightfully ours to begin with.

"I deserved the promotion." But what was the source of the original job opportunity that allowed you to learn the business and excel?

"Remember the LORD your God, for it is he who gives you the ability to produce."

"I got myself in shape." But what is the source of your fundamental health that allows you to have breath in your lungs to even get out of bed this morning?

"Remember the LORD your God, for it is he who gives you the ability to produce."

"I earned my degree." But what is the source of the wisdom and intellect that allowed you to complete your curriculum and field of study?

"Remember the LORD your God, for it is he who gives you the ability to produce."

When we really stop to think about it, we will come to a very humbling realization. The pride of production is all a fallacy. We really cannot take credit for anything we've "produced" in this life.

It is God who gives us the ability to produce. Do you "remember" him?

Have you worked hard? Certainly—and you should. Have you earned your successes along the way? Absolutely—and you must. I don't mean to minimize your dedication, commitment, and efforts. You've excelled. You've done well.

But ultimately, none of it—awards, accomplishments, achievement, recognition, wealth—is truly your own.

God created you with your talents. God made you with your abilities. God gave you your opportunities. God has mapped the perfect plan for your life. God is the source of it all. He is the ultimate producer.

How often do you "remember" him?

This week, take some time to praise the One "who gives you the ability to produce." Come before him with a heart filled to overflowing with gratitude. We are blessed beyond measure to even have a heartbeat when we wake up each morning, let alone to enjoy the many blessings of life that we've been given. Don't fall victim to the pride of production. Instead, "remember" your Heavenly Father, the ultimate producer and the source of "every good and perfect gift" (James 1:17).

THIS WEEK, STRIVE...

☐ To honestly acknowledge an accomplishment or area of your life where you've been hogging the credit. It could be something you made or achieved, or something for which others give you recognition. Own your pride of production.

☐ To ask for God's forgiveness for your pride of production. Admit to him you've taken credit for an accomplishment when he gave you the ability and the opportunity in the first place. Ask him for his help in enabling you to see all he's given you.

☐ To move from repentance to praise. Give God the credit he's due. Thank him that he's the source of all you've achieved and every blessing you've been graciously given. Remember him in all you do!

WE > ME
WEEK 14

*And you will again see the distinction between the righteous and the
wicked, between those who serve God and those who do not.*

MALACHI 3:18

I've often struggled with how to handle public recognition for acts of
service. Albeit a kind gesture to honor someone's generosity, it also tends
to elevate that individual above those in need.

During my time as a head football coach, I asked all of our players
to participate in several community service initiatives, and our program
got a lot of positive notoriety for it. Companies everywhere are embracing
"social responsibility" by giving time and money to support philanthropic
initiatives. The public's response and engagement has been tremendous.
Church websites and literature are full of content outlining the congre-
gation's generosity and service to those in need, and it is helping attract
and retain church members.

During my college football career I received several awards—one at
the national level—for the service and ministry work I performed as a
student-athlete. It was a tremendous honor that was extremely gratifying
and humbling to receive. But I couldn't help but be a little embarrassed
by the recognition. After all, as a Christian, isn't service-based ministry
what I'm supposed to be doing? Isn't that God's basic expectation of me?
I'm supposed to show up to work on time every day, and I don't get a
trophy for it. It's just expected. Why is this any different?

While this service makes a difference in the lives of others, at its core
is a fundamental question: Why are we serving?

Are we serving others to support them or for personal recognition? Are
we raising funds for a cause to help others or for personal satisfaction? Are
we doing charitable work to benefit the community or to advance ourselves?

Inner motives can be healthy, or they can be dangerous and self-serving. Righteous versus wicked; we versus me.

Malachi 3:18 tells us there is a clear "distinction between the righteous and the wicked, between those who serve God and those who do not." And what is the difference? We see it in our society every day.

The *righteous* are those who disadvantage themselves for the community. We first.

The *wicked* are those who disadvantage the community for themselves. Me first.

The Bible calls Noah a "righteous man" (Genesis 6:9). Scholars believe Noah spent fifty-five to seventy-five years inconveniencing himself to build the ark, following God's every directive in order to benefit future generations he would never even meet or know. Willingly, Noah disadvantaged himself for the benefit of the community of God's people. We first.

The Bible calls Nabal a "wicked man" (1 Samuel 25:25). You may never have heard of him; he's not exactly a biblical legend and for good reason. When King David and his men exit the wilderness of the Desert of Paran, they come to Nabal asking for food, drink, and a place to rest. But Nabal selfishly denies them in their need, saying all his goods are for him and his servants (1 Samuel 25:10-11). Selfishly, Nabal disadvantaged the community for his own benefit and gain. Me first.

I wonder how often we are Noah. I wonder how often we are Nabal.

If we're brutally honest with ourselves, our inner Nabal probably wins more often than we care to admit. Our inner me-first wickedness tends to rear its ugly head. Our *me* tends to be greater than (>) our *we*. Our sinful minds are programmed to take the path of least resistance.

easy > hard
comfort > inconvenience
safe > sacrifice
gain > giving
me > we

For the rest of the week, with God's help, let's snuff out our inner Nabal. Let's unleash our inner Noah. No more wickedness. No more self-serving behavior. Let's not think less of ourselves, but *let's think of ourselves less*. Let's recalibrate our thinking: we > me.

May the fruit of our life make the **"distinction between the righteous and the wicked"** crystal clear to a watching world. Let's live we > me!

THIS WEEK, STRIVE...

☐ To make a list of five things in your life where *me* > we. Five areas where you tend to be self-centered and put yourself ahead of others. Is it with your calendar? Is it with your wallet or budget? Where do you find it difficult to live sacrificially?

☐ To select one area of life on your list that you will move from *me* > we to *we* > me. What will you focus on? Where will you improve? It might be helpful to write it down.

☐ To list the steps you will take to make your *we* > me practice reality. Will you volunteer your time weekly? Will you review your budget weekly to monitor your giving progress? How will you accomplish your goal?

CLOSETS
WEEK 15

For the word of God is alive and active. Sharper than any double-edged sword, it penetrates even to dividing soul and spirit, joints and marrow; it judges the thoughts and attitudes of the heart. Nothing in all creation is hidden from God's sight. Everything is uncovered and laid bare before the eyes of him to whom we must give account.

HEBREWS 4:12–13

As a busy season of work and graduate school came to a close, I looked forward to once again seizing control of my weekend and evening schedule. I would have more time to devote to my love of physical fitness; I could read books of my choosing (not of my professors'!), and spend my time the way I wanted to spend it. I had long been looking forward to this day.

Little did I know that my wife also had been looking forward to this day. And her anticipation came with a little something extra: a to-do list. One project on the list was new carpeting in several rooms of our home. In prior months we had painted virtually every room in the house, but in order to take on this larger project, a few unpainted spaces had to be finished—in our closets.

Closets?

"This will be easy," I muttered to myself. "Be done in less than an hour."

Closets. Small spaces. No one sees them. A perfect paint job was not necessary. "This will be a cinch," I confidently thought. Little did I know how wrong I was.

Two hours and about a thousand negative thoughts, chiding comments, and loud sighs later, I was still not done with the smallest of the three closets I was painting.

There were tiny nooks and crannies filled with cobwebs to clean.

The angles of the small space were difficult to navigate without touching wet paint or bumping my head. My neck and back ached from arching around a shelf in the tiny crevice to clean and paint every square inch. It was an older home, and there was no light in this closet to see if I had adequately painted the corners.

Closets. As a more seasoned homeowner would later share with me, "Painting closets is the pits."

The house of our lives, in most cases, appears neat and tidy to a visitor's eye. The landscaping is impeccable. The décor is elegant. The floor plan is perfectly designed. Any visitor into our house of life will undoubtedly say, "Now this...this is a beautiful home." Anything and everything we are proud of, or that is visually pleasing, or that enhances our home, is prominently displayed. Anything that isn't goes in a closet. Visitors don't look in closets.

And like me and my closet-painting rendezvous, most homeowners don't think twice about closets unless absolutely necessary.

What closets in your life need cleaning and repainting? No Christ follower is exempt from the closets of life. We would be remiss to think otherwise. In these small, dark storage places of our lives we stockpile a host of things we hope the world never sees. Ugly attitudes are harbored. Greed runs amuck. Foul comments are prominent. Laziness is prevalent. Grudges are in the corner. Hurtful words are on the shelf. Inflated pride and egotistical thinking hangs on each hook and hanger.

Closets can be an ugly place. And in this life, these over-stocked, under-maintained little spaces can be a nasty reminder of the condition of our hearts, so we guard them tightly in an effort to hide what is really inside of us. No one can see our closets except our great God. Before our God and his word, there is nowhere to hide. Not even a closet.

We all need to do some daily closet cleaning with our Heavenly Father. And, as the author of Hebrews reminds us in our opening verse, there is nothing more cleansing for life's dingy closets than the word of God. Before God and his "penetrating" word every poor attitude is revealed, every flaw is exposed, every ego is humbled, and every darkness is brought into the light.

Like this overconfident homeowner, your life's closet cleaning will probably also yield some complaining, pain, and frustration. It will probably take longer than you thought it would. And it probably won't be nearly as easy as anticipated. But it will be well worth it.

Take some time this week to clean and repaint with God. Spend time in prayer, asking God to reveal the closet areas in your life. As you read his word, pray for the Holy Spirit to expose the things in your life's closet that are holding you back from a greater impact for his Kingdom. The process will likely be humbling and uncomfortable. But, like our carpet project, you may have to clean your closets first in order for God to use you to complete a larger endeavor for his Kingdom.

Sometimes he must change us in order to use us to change others. His biggest plans for you are yet to come!

THIS WEEK, STRIVE…

- ☐ To think through all the things that are in your life's closet. What's in there? Hidden habits? Past regrets? Anger or hatred? Why do you keep it tucked away?
- ☐ To pick one thing from your life's closet that you want to get rid of. What's the one thing you've kept tucked away that you know needs to go? You won't empty out your closet in a day. This will take time. Pray for God's guidance in selecting what you will discard.
- ☐ To pray every day this week for God's guidance, strength, and support as you move what you've selected out of your dark closet and into his light. Stay persistent in prayer. Be patient. Trust his plan. Don't hide anymore. Entrust it to God!

Too Much
Week 16

Endure hardship as discipline; God is treating you as his children. For what children are not disciplined by their father?

HEBREWS 12:7

Too many good things can actually be a bad thing.

During the summer of 2012, the entire United States experienced extended periods of hot temperatures, dry conditions, and drought. Not good for agricultural production at all.

Except for grapes. Wineries and vineyards across the US and Canada had exceptional years.

How can this possibly be? Too much good is bad for grapes.

Even in normal conditions with normal amounts of rain, vineyard farmers purposely expose grapes to dry conditions. The stress is good for the fruit. A grape that receives too much water is smaller, often discolored, and sour.[1] If exposed to too much water over time, the excess moisture entering the vine can cause the grapes to start rotting from the inside. The adversity of lacking water forces the vine to drive its roots down deeper into the soil for both water and nutrients. The result is a larger, full colored, juicier, better tasting grape.

Too much good is bad. The same is true in our own lives. Like grapes in a dry field being prepared for a great crop, so too God exposes us to the adversity of "drought" to produce in us fruit for his Kingdom. Hebrews 12:7–11 tells us:

> Endure hardship as discipline; God is treating you as his children. For what children are not disciplined by their father? If you are not disciplined—and everyone undergoes discipline— then you are not legitimate, not true sons and daughters at all.

Moreover, we have all had human fathers who disciplined us and we respected them for it. How much more should we submit to the Father of spirit and live! They disciplined us for a little while as they thought best; but God disciplines us for our good, in order that we may share in his holiness. No discipline seems pleasant at the time, but painful. Later on, however, it produces a harvest of righteousness and peace for those who have been trained by it.

We must remember three things when we find ourselves in hardship:

1. HARDSHIP IS EDUCATIONAL

Anyone who is a parent understands Hebrews' parallel to parental discipline. Like a parent who disciplines a child in the child's best interest and to teach the child something, so too God uses hardship to teach us. In the midst of trials, we must not ask, "God, how do I get out of this?" but rather, "God what do you want me to get out of this?"

2. HARDSHIP IS TEMPORARY

"No discipline seems pleasant at the time, but painful." "At the time" means that all hardship comes to an end. Some hardship ends here on earth during our lifetime. But all hardship ends when we meet our Maker eternally (Praise God!). Hold fast—your hardships will not last!

3. HARDSHIP IS PRODUCTIVE (IF WE ALLOW IT TO BE!)

"Later on, however, it produces a harvest of righteousness and peace for those who have been trained by it." This verse can be true if we are willing to be two things—patient ("Later on") and humble ("trained by it"). Patient humility allows hardship to produce "righteousness and peace" in us for God's Kingdom.

This week, whatever hardship, adversity, or "drought" you are facing, look past your circumstances to the outcome—God's perfect outcome for your life. Too much good truly is bad for our spiritual growth. If we view hardship as educational, temporary, and productive, God can use us for greater good than we ever imagined.

God is in complete control, and if you'll allow him (patience and humility), he will mold you into all you are designed to become!

THIS WEEK, STRIVE...

- ☐ To memorize Hebrews 12:11. Commit it to memory through reading, writing, and reciting it each day this week.
- ☐ To apply Hebrews 12:11 to a drought in your life. How can this drought "train" you? Consider or list out the "harvest of righteousness and peace" that could come out of your drought if you allow it.
- ☐ To pray for God's strength, along with an open mind, to face your drought with courage and to learn from its teachable moments. How will you grow through this adversity?

At that time Abijah son of Jeroboam became ill, and Jeroboam said to his wife, "Go, disguise yourself, so you won't be recognized as the wife of Jeroboam. Then go to Shiloh. Ahijah the prophet is there—the one who told me I would be king over this people. ...So Jeroboam's wife did what he said and went to Ahijah's house in Shiloh. Now Ahijah could not see; his sight was gone because of his age. But the Lord had told Ahijah, "Jeroboam's wife is coming to ask you about her son, for he is ill, and you are to give her such and such an answer. When she arrives, she will pretend to be someone else." So when Ahijah heard the sound of her footsteps at the door, he said, "Come in, wife of Jeroboam. Why this pretense?"

1 Kings 14:1–6

During my time in the National Football League, I came to find that each locker room had its fair share of disguises—things used to conceal true identity.

These disguises took on varying forms. Sometimes it was a financial disguise, as younger players would throw away thousands of dollars (that's right, I said thousands) on high stakes card games between practices or meetings, in an effort to keep pace with the veteran players' bets. Sometimes it was a relational disguise, as married men would charm and entice flight attendants or hotel staff on road trips. Sometimes it was a toughness disguise, as a handful of players and coaches would constantly carry themselves with a cold, hard outer veneer in order to garner the reputation of being a force to be reckoned with, on and off the field.

But disguises are not limited to professional athletes by any stretch of the imagination. They're all around us each day.

We create the disguise of prosperity by mortgaging and borrowing up to our eyeballs in order to have the biggest house or the nicest car. We create the disguise of superior knowledge by speaking a certain way or name-dropping our contacts to others. Nowadays, we even create the disguise of being another person, as social media and dating websites provide the ability to be someone we're not from behind the disguise of a monitor and keyboard.

But disguises also run much deeper than what we have, what we know, or who we wish we were as a person. They impact our daily life. We create the disguise of inner peace, when we truly have no peace at all. We create the disguise of joy, when we feel discouraged and lifeless. We create the disguise of love, when inside we feel bitter and angry.

Worst of all, we create the disguise of righteousness to cover up our sin.

Sadly, I have put on a couple of these aforementioned disguises in my own life, and I'm sure you have too. As I reflect on those disguises, all I can think about is: how silly. God knows all. He can see right through any disguise.

King Jeroboam and his wife found this out the hard way. After King Solomon's reign ended in sin and disobedience, God tore the majority of the rule of Israel away from David's lineage. Israel became split into two kingdoms—Israel and Judah.

Jeroboam ruled the kingdom of Israel for a little over twenty years. But he ruled in a sinful manner, displeasing to God. As a result, Jeroboam's sin fell on the rest of his family and household—as predicted to Jeroboam by an unnamed prophet in 1 Kings 13.

One of the side effects of this sin was the illness of his son Abijah. In a panic and wanting to conceal the appearance of any weakness, pain, or suffering from the house of the king, Jeroboam sends his wife in disguise to Ahijah the prophet, hoping he can provide some sort of answer for his son's illness.

But we see through Ahijah that "The Lord does not look at the things people look at. People look at the outward appearance, but the Lord looks at the heart" (1 Samuel 16:7).

Ahijah, warned by God about the disguise, sees right through the smoke and mirrors—despite his blindness! (Just goes to show how effective our disguises are before God!) But he does not judge or condemn Jeroboam's wife. He invites her in—"Come in, wife of Jeroboam. Why this pretense?"—and he then presents her with some hard truth about the fate of her son and family.

Which is exactly what God will do if we let him. He will invite us in and tell us the truth about who we are.

"Come in, (*your name here*). Why this pretense? Take off your disguises. Let me show you who you really are!"

Today, throw off your disguises. God sees right through them anyway. Be yourself, for he made you for a divine purpose. Come to your Maker. He will not judge you or condemn you. He will tell you the truth about who you are and whose you are. You are his! And that need not be disguised!

THIS WEEK, STRIVE...

- ☐ To identify one disguise you put on most often. What is one area where who you genuinely are might not match up with the way you think, act, or speak? Are you a people pleaser? Do you behave a certain way to fit in with the crowd you're with? Is there something inside you're hiding with outward appearance? Whatever it is, take responsibility for your disguise.
- ☐ To read Galatians 3:26-4:7 at least twice this week. What does it say about our true identity?
- ☐ To pray daily that God would mold you into who he desires you to be, not just who you desire to be. It won't be easy, but with his help, what are some first steps you can take this week to put off your disguises and live into your true identity in Christ?

THE CANCER OF ENTITLEMENT
WEEK 18

The LORD did not set his affection on you and choose you because you were more numerous than other peoples, for you were the fewest of all peoples.

DEUTERONOMY 7:7

There's a problem in our world today that is driving me nuts, so I've decided to call everyone reading this to the carpet.

You've been warned.

I'm starting by calling my generation, and the generation of young people after me, into the spotlight (I'm a Gen Y-er, or "millennial," born in 1986) because we are the worst culprits of the problem permeating throughout society. And the primary responsibility for future change lies in our capable hands.

But I'm also calling the bluff of those generations that have come before us, because you play a critical role in developing the leaders of tomorrow. The up-and-comers need the mentorship and guidance of our current leaders to change the trajectory of our society for the better.

So what's the big issue of which I speak? Entitlement. We think we deserve certain things. No one is immune. We all do this, but especially our youth. And it's getting worse.

Don't believe me? An article I recently read said that Ivy League faculty and staff are reporting they've heard the following comments from their students:

- "I pay your salary, so you have to do what I want."
- "Why didn't I get an A? I showed up to class every day."
- "So I failed the test. What do I need to do to get the grade I want?"

- "This guarantees me a job, right?"
- "If my parents are paying my tuition, I deserve a better grade."
- "You can't criticize me. I tried."[1]

If that isn't enough, consider this study conducted at the University of California at Berkeley. The researchers placed groups of students into teams of three, separated by gender, and put each team into a different room. The researchers entered the room and randomly selected one of the three people to be the team's "leader." Then the researchers gave the team a complicated campus moral issue—like plagiarism or underage alcohol consumption—to solve.

Thirty minutes into each team's discussion, the researchers barged into each room unannounced and brought in a plate of cookies. But instead of three cookies, there were four cookies on the plate. Everyone got a cookie. But what about the fourth?

Awkward situation. Especially with three random people who don't know each other. Right?

Wrong.

In each team, the randomly selected leader ate the fourth cookie. The leader hadn't done anything special. He or she hadn't even taken command of the group in many cases but had been haphazardly named as the leader. Yet each felt entitled to the extra cookie.[2]

The cancer of entitlement is permeating our world. And because it is, entitlement is permeating our spiritual lives too.

"I've lived a good life. I haven't done anything all that wrong. I haven't committed any major sins. I'm in church. I put money in the offering plate. I'm a good person. . . ."

"So, God, you owe me something."

No he doesn't. God doesn't owe us anything.

Consider God's words to the chosen nation of Israel in Deuteronomy 7:7: "The Lord did not set his affection on you and choose you because you were more numerous than other peoples, for you were the fewest of all peoples." Israel was chosen, yet not deserving or entitled in any way.

Consider the life of Job, a man the Bible calls "blameless and upright," yet he experienced loss of loved ones, health, wealth, status and power, and nearly his life.

Consider the Apostle Paul, one of the most faithful Gospel spreaders to ever walk the earth. Yet he had to endure flogging, beating, stoning, shipwrecks, homelessness, danger, starvation, and sleeplessness (see 2 Corinthians 11:21–33).

Faithfulness to God doesn't mean we get what we want or what we think we deserve. God doesn't owe us anything. We owe him *everything* because he gave it all for us (see Isaiah 53:4–6).

Let's be men and women who work hard, count our blessings, and "in humility value others above [ourselves]" (Philippians 2:3) as we seek to unselfishly meet "the interests of the others" (v. 4) before our own. Let's all, collectively, be the people that cure the cancer of entitlement in our world!

THIS WEEK, STRIVE…

- ☐ To perform a pride/blessing inventory. Fold a sheet of paper into two columns. In the left hand column, list the accomplishments, relationships, possessions, and more that are sources of pride in your life.
- ☐ To now list all the blessings you can think of in the right hand column. List everything you can think of—faith, people, possessions, health, and more. Make the list as all-inclusive as possible.
- ☐ To compare your side-by-side lists. How many of your sources of pride were due to the investment of others? How many blessings were things you didn't deserve or ask for but were generous gifts or opportunities? How do blessings balance pride? How can an attitude of gratitude combat entitlement in our world?

FOCUS
WEEK 19

"Martha, Martha," the Lord answered, "You are worried and upset about many things, but few things are needed—or indeed only one. Mary has chosen what is better, and it will not be taken away from her."

LUKE 10:41–42

New opportunities are great. But invariably, each comes with a big issue. A focus issue.

Being an NFL rookie meant the opportunity of a lifetime was before me, something I'd dreamt of and worked for over the course of months and years. But with it came a host of things to address: finalizing contract negotiations, developing relationships with teammates and coaches, packing up and moving to a new city, finding a place to live, learning the new offense—and that was only the beginning! Where was I to even start?

Entering the world of being a high school head football coach was another exciting opportunity. I began the new post in February 2011. In fact, my first day on the job was exactly 180 days before our first game. I know that sounds like a long time. But trust me, it isn't. In that short window of time I needed to hire a coaching staff, develop and implement the strength-and-conditioning program, develop relationships with players, evaluate talent, implement offensive, defensive, and special-teams systems, structure the budget, set the plan for summer camps, and many more vital tasks! How was I going to figure everything out?

Most recently, I found myself transitioning into a new role at work in the corporate world and once again being thrust into the slew of new things to figure out. From learning the dynamics of a new group of people around me to understanding the complexities of the problem I was called on to solve and developing a plan to resolve the issue—the demands were the same: overwhelming!

Even in my personal life and walk with Jesus Christ, I find myself bombarded with new opportunities to partner with ministries, donate to great organizations, or volunteer my time. Every one of them is seeking to do good in the world, to serve others, and further God's Kingdom here on earth. How am I to decide where to commit myself?

In some form, you've been in these situations before too—from your first day at school, to moving your family, to starting a new job, to becoming a new parent, to requests to give of your time, talent, and treasure. In some way, you know what it feels like to be pulled a million different directions. You've stepped back and asked yourself: Where do I even begin? How will I ever figure this out? What are the best ways for me to give of myself?

New opportunities are exciting. But they are also a lot like trying to catch the rain with a funnel. They challenge our ability to focus. They crowd our capacity to put our best energy and effort toward what is most important. If we aren't careful, they can leave us chasing things that matter least, while we neglect the very things that matter most.

What are we to do? How do we keep first things first? How do we refrain from chasing hollow busyness and meaningless pursuits? How do we keep from losing our focus?

I'm convinced we will not find a better answer to this question than the one Jesus presents in the account of two sisters—Mary and Martha— found in Luke's gospel account.

These sisters were faced with a new opportunity as well: to hear the rising star of their day—Jesus of Nazareth—teach to their friends and family. His teaching wasn't like the pharisaical religious leaders of the day, filled with legalism and condescension. His teaching was different— spoken with powerful authority yet filled with genuine love and concern. But not only would Mary and Martha hear Jesus teach, they were about to host him in their home!

Picture the situation for a moment. Put yourself there. The celebrity or public figure you'd most like to meet—more than anyone else in the entire world—is coming to your house! What would you do?

You'd probably be concerned about making a great impression on your admired guest. You'd want to roll out the figurative red carpet. With a long to-do list of preparations, you would likely ask some family members, like your sister, to help you get ready. You'd be busy scurrying around cooking, cleaning, decorating, hosting, and making sure everything is perfect.

You'd probably have focus issues, like Martha. The story calls her "distracted." That's what new opportunities have the potential to do.

In a tizzy from her lack of focus, Martha realizes she can't find her sister anywhere, the sister who was supposed to be helping her. Martha stomps off, making a brisk lap through the house with heavy heels and a short fuse.

Martha finds Mary sitting at the feet of Jesus, not missing a moment of his visit, hanging on every word, enjoying his presence, spending invaluable time with him.

I can see Martha gripping her dirty apron as she can't hold it in anymore. "Lord, don't you care that my sister has left me to do the work by myself? Tell her to help me!" (Luke 10:40).

Calmly yet clearly, Jesus lays out the way—to Martha and to us—that we keep from losing focus in our lives.

1. FEW THINGS ARE NEEDED

New opportunities are great, but a disciplined pursuit of less will keep us focused and make the greatest impact. The more we take on, the more we tend to grow "worried and upset about many things," and the less effective we become. It is essential that we prayerfully consider the question—Where can I best use my gifts to *meet needs*?—and that we align our commitments around the answer.

2. ONE THING IS BETTER THAN THE REST

God's word is not shy about claiming exclusivity in our lives. No matter how much we do, give, and serve, a personal relationship with Jesus Christ is supreme. The psalmist writes that "The earth is the LORD's, and everything in it" (Psalm 24:1). Jesus identified himself as "the way and the truth and the life" (John 14:6). A *focused* Mary spending time with Jesus, is far better than a busy Martha, who ignores God's presence. Is your faith a part of all you do? Is it your *main focus* in everything you take on?

3. WHAT WE CHOOSE HAS LASTING IMPLICATIONS

The things we choose to *focus* on in this life have repercussions for all eternity. Little did Mary know, but more than two thousand years later, millions and millions of Bible readers have learned from her practical example to focus on Jesus over the busyness of the world. As Jesus predicted, Mary's conscious decision to focus on him would "not be taken away from her." Are you choosing wisely? What lasting impact will the choices you make today have?

This week, let's concentrate on the few ways God desires to use us to meet needs and ensure that our relationship with his son Jesus is above all else in our daily lives. Let's remember the powerful and eternal effects of the choices we make today. While we are grateful for the new opportunities that come our way, let's allow nothing to rob of us of our focus!

THIS WEEK, STRIVE...

- ☐ To spend some time evaluating the way you make decisions. I'm sure you gather lots of information and think things through. You probably gather the opinions of several people you trust. But do you ever ask God, "What do you want, Lord?" Is he a key input to making your decisions? Is he first in your process? Do you need to change the way you make decisions?
- ☐ To consider the ease with which you are able to say no to things. Does it come easily to you or is it difficult? Do you feel pressure to say yes and the judgment of others if you say no? How can

you be better at saying no to good things so you can say yes to the best things?

☐ To come up with a strategy to integrate your faith in Christ into the things that take up the largest share of your time. List the top three things that consume the most time in your schedule—work, family, friends, church, volunteer work, fitness, and so forth. Then under each item, write two ways you can integrate your relationship with Christ into that endeavor. (Example – under fitness, you might write: "Invite Bill from the gym to church.") What excites you about your strategy? What will be challenging?

THE DANGER (AND BLESSING) OF IMITATION
WEEK 20

Do not be misled: "Bad company corrupts good character."

1 CORINTHIANS 15:33

During my short time in professional football, I was blessed with the rare opportunity to be around some of the very best quarterbacks to ever play the game. And while the coaching was top notch as well, there were times when giving directives to us back-up quarterbacks was very, very easy, especially in Indianapolis.

"You see how Peyton did that? Imitate him."

We heard this on a weekly basis. From voice inflection during the cadence, to command of the huddle, to footwork, to the rhythm of how we audibled, there truly was no one better to mimic than number 18.

Imitation is the propensity to observe and then replicate the behavior of another. Psychologists have found that our human minds are filled with mirror neurons that stand ready to fire when we observe similar actions performed by someone or something else.

In short, we are prone and trained to imitate. There really isn't a better way to learn.

Imitation is key in our early development. From birth to two years old, babies are in their sensorimotor stage of development—meaning they are learning by imitating observed actions. (No pressure, parents!)

Imitation is how culture, innovation, and tradition is passed on from generation to generation. It's how customs form, advancement occurs, and society keeps moving forward.

Imitation helps write the story of this life. It can be a very good thing. It can also be bad.

Imitation is also a part of social learning. Our tendency to imitate manifests itself in our communal and societal relationships. Our friends and family influence us deeply! Psychologists have found that a human being will behave like the three people with whom he or she engages most. In the words of motivational speaker and author Jim Rohn, "You are the average of the five people you spend the most time with."

Reading this information, some of you are happy right now. Some of you are saying, "Yes, I know this. Please go on."

Some of you are seeing necessary change on the horizon. Some of you are saying, "I can't hang out with him anymore."

Our inclination to imitate reveals a vital fact: We must surround ourselves with the quality people and cultivate wise friendships.

Proverbs 17:17 captures this powerful principle of wise friendship: "A friend loves at all times, and a brother is born for a time of adversity."

Now that's the type of friend we are searching for! Someone loyal, trustworthy, and true. Someone who cares about us, who we can spend time with and are proud to call a friend. Someone we can confidently imitate.

We all need friends in this life who are worthy of imitation. For me, this friend is a former teammate who I can always count on. We can get in God's word and pray together. We can hold each other accountable. We can have tough conversations about our successes and our struggles. And I always know that he is living his life in a manner that honors Jesus.

But despite the blessing of our earthly friends, I believe the author of Proverbs 17 was also foreshadowing another loyal comrade who was to come. Who was this friend?

Jesus Christ, the son of the Most High God.

How do we become his friend?

Oddly enough, by imitation. Jesus makes this explicitly clear in John 15:14: "You are my friends if you do what I command."

Read his word. Study his teachings. Give it a chance to soak in. Apply it to your life. Then imitate it. Do what he commands. And when you do, you'll have a "friend that sticks closer than a brother."

Today, take a few moments to do a relationship inventory. Who are the three to five people you are spending the most time with? How's their influence on you? Is it making you a better person? Are they worthy of imitation?

Then turn your eyes to the One worthy of imitation—Jesus the Messiah. He is the true friend!

THIS WEEK, STRIVE...

- ☐ To list the top five people you spend the most time with each week. Does your list surprise you? Are these people worthy of imitation? Any changes you need to make?
- ☐ To do some people watching. Study those around you as you live, work, and go about your business. Listen to what they say. Watch how they conduct themselves. Who is worthy of imitation? Make mental notes. Then seek out an opportunity to get to know this person. Should you add them to your list of three to five people to spend time with?
- ☐ To spend time in prayer with the ultimate friend, Jesus, each day before you eat breakfast. No Jesus, no breakfast. If you don't eat breakfast, then don't start your work or the first item on your agenda without coming to him in prayer. Start the day out right—with the One worthy of imitation!

HUMBITION
WEEK 21

Wisdom's instruction is to fear the LORD, and humility comes before honor.

PROVERBS 15:33

Before a downfall the heart is haughty, but humility comes before honor.

PROVERBS 18:12

Today's young people are growing up and entering the "real world." But as they do so, they bring an entirely different context to the workforce, a context filled with technology inundation, instant gratification, and social media significance, a belief that they can be productive employees right away. There is one thing they surely possess: ambition. Consider the following findings:[1]

- An overwhelming 93 percent of millennials say they want a job where they can be themselves at work, and that includes dressing in a way that makes them comfortable.
- Research shows that 81 percent of millennials think they should be allowed to make their own hours at work.
- More than nine in ten millennials want supervisors, managers, and executives to listen to their ideas.
- Seventy-six percent of millennials think their bosses could learn a lot from them.

Ambition is great. It accomplishes things and projects confidence. Ambition is driven, works hard, is creative, and doesn't settle for second best. It sets goals and then pursues those goals relentlessly. Ambition desires significance.

But there's something missing in this list of young people's desires for their careers. In fact, there's something missing in most of the world's desires these days: humility.

Humility says, "There might be other ways to do things besides my way." Humility listens first before acting, is slow to speak, knows that it doesn't know everything, and is willing to learn. Humility leads by example.

At the core of ambition is a desire to achieve, to make an impact on something or someone, and to be significant. But the Bible is very clear about the proper order of things: "Humility comes before honor."

Learning before climbing the ladder. Sacrifice before significance. Listening before directing. Perseverance before progress. Patience before being rewarded. *Humility before honor.*

Our world doesn't like this. It wants things the other way around. Recognition now. Promotion today. Instant impact. Immediate results.

It just doesn't work that way. Humility comes before honor.

But maybe we can find balance. Maybe we can have our cake and eat it too.

HUMILITY + AMBITION = *HUMBITION*

What if we all balanced our ambition with humility? What if we quietly showed how much we know rather than talking about it? What if we listened to direction and carried it out to the best of our abilities— then earning the right to lead and give the direction in the future? What if we selflessly advanced God's agenda rather than our own?

What if we all lived with *humbition?*

I bet we'd all accomplish more, have better relationships, and be better listeners. We would learn more than we ever thought we would, our minds would be more open, and we'd all be more unselfish.

I bet God would receive more glory, and we would hog less for ourselves. And that's the way it should be.

This week, let's test it out. Let's show the world humble ambition—*humbition*. Let's remember that humility comes before honor. In all we think, say, and do, let's exude the character of Jesus Christ to a watching world. May the glory be his, not ours!

THIS WEEK, STRIVE...

☐ To capture your three greatest ambitions, the three things you are pursuing that occupy your mind and your time. They could be work related, relationship oriented, faith based, or from your bucket list. Write them down on a post-it note, record them on your phone or tablet, and put them somewhere you will see them often this week.

☐ To prayerfully consider where pride is slowing the accomplishment of your top three ambitions. Maybe learning more on a subject will propel you toward an ambition. Maybe putting your own agenda aside will improve a relationship ambition. Maybe your need to control is keeping you from your ambition to trust God more. Pray into the pride issues you dig up this week. Ask for God to illuminate areas where you can exercise more humility.

☐ To memorize Proverbs 15:33: "Wisdom's instruction is to fear the Lord, and humility comes before honor." How will living with humbition make you go further more quickly this week as you Strive toward your top three ambitions?

Defining Moments
Week 22

Ahab said to Naboth, "Let me have your vineyard to use for a veg-
etable garden, since it is close to my palace." ...But Naboth replied,
"The Lord forbid that I should give you the inheritance of my ances-
tors." So Ahab went home, sullen and angry because Naboth the
Jezreelite had said, "I will not give you the inheritance of my ances-
tors." He lay on his bed sulking and refused to eat.... Jezebel his wife
said, "Is this how you act as king over Israel? Get up and eat! Cheer
up."

1 Kings 21:2–7

This was it. The culmination of everything for which I had been working:
final NFL roster cuts.

After years of dodging imaginary defenders in the back yard, cutting
out pictures from *Sports Illustrated for Kids*, and dreaming about stardom;
of learning through youth and middle school football, of dedication and
effort to excel in high school, and of hard work to break into the college
lineup and to play at a high level; of the agent selection process, the grind
of training twice a day, six days a week to prepare for all-star games, the
NFL combine, pro-day workouts, and team pre-draft interviews; the
months of long hours in the film room, at mini-camp, in the weight
room, and at organized team activities; the mental and physical grind of
an NFL training camp and four preseason games as a final proving
ground—it all came down to this moment.

"We're going to have to let you go."

For a born-again Christian, these are defining moments.

You've been faithful to God. You're studying and living by his word.
You're faithfully engaged in intimate prayer. You've been using your gifts
and talents to serve him. You've been kind to others, showing them his

mercy and love. You're generously giving of your resources to God's work in the world. You're active in your church and small group, seeking to grow in faith.

But the results come in:

"We're going to take our business elsewhere."

"We're going to be eliminating your position."

"The surgery didn't work as well as we planned."

"I'm sorry, but the cancer is back again."

"There's been an accident. It's your son."

How do you respond when you don't get what you want? When what you want and God's will for your life don't quite match up? Is God suddenly not good? Is he not all-knowing? Is he not all-loving? Is he not full of grace? Is he no longer in control? Does he no longer have a perfect plan for your life?

Has he suddenly changed because you didn't get your way? How do you respond when your plans crumble? What do you do when your way doesn't come to fruition?

That, my friends, is the true test. The defining moment of your faith. What will you do?

Will you be like King Ahab? Bitter, sour, and filled with resentment? Denied the vineyard land that he passionately wanted to own, he grew "sullen and angry" as "he lay on his bed sulking and refused to eat."

Or will you be like another King? Feeling fear and distress from not getting his way, this King came to his defining moment of faith. Denied his request in faithful prayer, this King became filled with trust and assurance that, though he wasn't getting what he wanted, God had a better plan than he could even imagine.

"Father, if you are willing, take this cup from me; yet not my will, but yours be done" (Luke 22:42).

King Jesus. Willing to trust God, even when He didn't get his way. even through Calvary's cross, even through death.

How will you respond when you don't get what you want? How will you handle your defining moment of faith?

Today, simply remember this—God always gives us what we would want if we knew everything he knows. Let's trust him completely as we take on life's defining moments!

THIS WEEK, STRIVE...

- ☐ To monitor your reactions to any bad news you receive this week. Bad news is a defining moment! Do you lash out? Roll your eyes? Make a face? Get angry? It sounds trivial, but your reaction sets your attitude toward the news. Seek to improve your response to tough situations.
- ☐ To identify one circumstance in your life that you don't like or understand. Write it down. Why are you discontent? List all the reasons you can think of below your circumstance.
- ☐ To pray over your circumstance and discontentments every day this week. Hold the sheet of paper as you pray. Pray the same prayer Jesus prayed in Luke 22:42: "Not my will, but yours be done." Make note of how your attitude and outlook change as you continually pray this prayer.

IDENTITY CRISIS
WEEK 23

Yet to all who did receive him, to those who believed in his name, he gave the right to become children of God—children born not of natural descent, nor of human decision or a husband's will, but born of God.

JOHN 1:12–13

"Mister... Umm, excuse me! Mister! Mister! Mister?"

I looked down toward the source of this frantic attention seeker. About four feet below, a five-year-old boy named Lenny was excitedly tugging on my shirt and poking me in the leg while dangling his full body weight from my right arm. On seeing he had finally captured my full attention, he stared back up at me with big, brown, curious eyes.

"Mister...what do you do?"

That question never really bothered me until that moment. I was in my wife's kindergarten classroom volunteering, fresh from being released from the roster of the Indianapolis Colts just a few weeks ago. I was embarrassed that I had been cut. I was ashamed of what I thought defined me as a failure. I was bottling up a lot of hurt.

Lenny's posed his question in complete and utter innocence. He probably asked me because my wife told the class a special guest was coming to visit. But it bothered me just the same.

I was going through an identity crisis. I had been playing football successfully at a high level for many years. I had invested an inordinate amount of work in my career. It had become a part of me. So much so, that I had allowed it to seep into the core of my being and my self-worth.

Football had become my identity. And we usually don't realize the thing that is defining our identity until that thing is taken away.

Think about meeting someone new at a social gathering. After introducing yourself, what's one of the first questions you ask?

"What do you do?"

It's ingrained in our nature and our culture: Drawing significance from our busyness. Finding value in our net worth. Seeking purpose in our productivity. Defining a person's substance, importance, and identity by the question, "What do you do?" It's even how a five-year-old begins conversation!

Our propensity to ask, "What do you do?" is a symptom of a far greater problem in our world, an epidemic of great proportions. We are in the midst of an identity crisis.

Our society, our culture, our world is sending a powerful message: You build who you are through what you do. You make an identity, fabricate a persona, and build a life through accomplishment, achievement, and accrual of power and resources. Success by significance!

Is that all there is? What if I fail? What if no one notices me? What if I miss the standard? Is that the end of the story?

No, thankfully. There is another story. A different story. The story of the Bible. Where our identity is already truly defined:

"Yet to all who did receive him, to those who believed in his name, he gave the right to become children of God."

While the world says you build who you are through what you do, the Bible teaches that who you are is already built in Christ. We are children of God! With our identity secure in Jesus, what we do is simply grateful stewardship of the gifts God has given us.

Success by sacrifice, and not of our own doing. Success by Christ's sacrifice.

The pressure is off! No longer do we need to build who we are through what we do! We are told who we are! If we believe "in his name" and in the price he paid for our sin, he gives us "the right to become children of God!" We can then freely use our God-given abilities to serve him, in grateful stewardship, through what we do.

Today, keep it simple! Trust God. Be you. Serve him!

THIS WEEK, STRIVE...

☐ To make an "identity list." Identify all the things in this life that make you feel important or worthwhile. List as many things as you can think of—people, possessions, accomplishments, and more—from which you draw identity or value.

☐ To read Philippians 2:1–11 at least twice. As you read it, make a similar identity list of the qualities or attributes of Jesus that you observe in these verses.

☐ To analyze your identity list side by side with the identity list of Jesus. Are there any similarities? Are there lots of discrepancies? Prayerfully resolve, with God's help, to find identity in him alone, and to imitate Jesus' identity list in your daily life.

He decreed statutes for Jacob and established the law in Israel, which he commanded our ancestors to teach their children, so the next generation would know them, even the children yet to be born, and they in turn would tell their children. Then they would put their trust in God and would not forget his deeds but would keep his commands.

PSALM 78:5–7

Consider a group of ten young, teenage Christ followers. Research shows that, of the ten:

- Four will wander away from the church.
- Three will stay faithful to church and to their faith.
- Two will say they feel "lost" between church and society.
- One will abandon the faith completely.[1]

If you're like me, after reading these alarming statistics, your mind searches for possible reasons for this data and solutions to solve the problem.

But then my mind went to a completely different place: *The Lorax*, by Dr. Seuss.

With my wife being a kindergarten teacher, I've found myself quite familiar with the storyline of this children's book. Consider the powerful message the Lorax leaves behind for the greedy, polluting, Truffula tree-chopping, Thneed-manufacturing Once-ler:

And all that the Lorax left here in this mess
was a small pile of rocks, with the one word…

"UNLESS."

Whatever that meant, well, I just couldn't guess.[2]

Unless.

In the English language, *unless* is a powerful word. It's a transition in a sentence, a tipping point, a fulcrum. Everything hinges on *unless*. It transforms what is, into what could be.

"The game will be lost *unless* they can make a comeback."

"We can't make that happen *unless* we hear some good news."

"She will die *unless* an organ donor is found."

"Only 30 percent of teens will continue following Jesus into adulthood *unless* we do something about it."

What are we to do?

Psalm 78 clearly communicates that God gave us his word not only to instruct us but also to share with the next generation, to raise them and train them in his ways. How does this passing on of God's word happen?

1. TEACH. ("He commanded our ancestors to teach their children, so the next generation would know" [vv. 5–6]).

Proverbs 22:6 wisely instructs, "Start children off on the way they should go, and even when they are old they will not turn from it." But the data shows that we are starting children on the right path, we just aren't finishing! The job of Christian parenting and mentoring doesn't end at age eighteen; it is an ongoing, life-long process of teachable moments. Using God's word as a guide for critical moments—handling failure, dealing with loss, nurturing appropriate relationships, pondering big decisions—leaves a lasting impression.

2. TELL. ("And they in turn would tell their children" [v. 6].)

Psalm 78 outlines a chain-reaction model. Leave an indelible imprint of Christ on a child and not only will the child never forget it, the child will pass it on to his or her children, who will then tell their children. One of the best ways to do this is through real-life stories. Being candid with young people about your successes, failures, and what God has taught you along the way. You'll be surprised how much they retain and apply.

2. MODEL. ("Then they would put their trust in God and would not forget his deeds but would keep his commands" [v. 7].)

Notice how the children will remember to keep God's commands: by "his deeds." We too can emulate God's actions and attitudes—his faithful love, his patient mercy, his forgiving spirit—in our daily lives. A picture is worth a thousand words, and today's youth need a picture of what men and women of Christ look like. There are few such pictures for them to see in our world today! Young people are not only observant, but they are eagerly watching, and this presents a rare and powerful opportunity for lasting impact that prepares them to be sent out as Christian leaders into our broken world!

Today, take on the challenge of Dr. Seuss's Once-ler from the final page of The Lorax:

"But now," says the Once-ler,
"Now that you're here,
the word of the Lorax seems perfectly clear.
UNLESS someone like you
cares a whole awful lot,
nothing is going to get better.
It's not."[2]

Teach, tell, and model Jesus Christ for the next generation. Things are not going to get better unless we do!

THIS WEEK, STRIVE...

☐ To write down one lesson you would like to teach to someone who may follow in your footsteps one day. What do they need to know?

☐ To write down names of those with whom you could share the lessons you've learned. Whom will you tell? Who needs to hear what you have learned along the way?

☐ To write down how you will model the things you've learned for those you can impact around you. What do they need to see in your life? How can you be a mentor and an example?

KEEP SAYING IT
WEEK 25

The next day John saw Jesus coming toward him and said, "Look, the Lamb of God, who takes away the sin of the world! ...I have seen and I testify that this is God's Chosen One." The next day John was there again with two of his disciples. When he saw Jesus passing by, he said, "Look, the Lamb of God!" When the two disciples heard him say this, they followed Jesus.

JOHN 1:29–37

The Rule of Seven is an axiom of social psychology that, whether true or not, seems to have withstood the test of time. It states that an individual must hear or see a message at least seven times before it sinks in and he or she takes action. In the business sense, before a consumer makes a purchase decision. In the academic sense, before a student will put learning into practice.

I found this especially true as a young football coach. When you get your first opportunity to lead a program, you're filled with ideas and fervor. You want to accomplish everything under the sun, and you want to do it now.

But the reality is, you must select two or three key things you want your players to exemplify and hammer them home. You must talk about them constantly and live them out yourself. You must post them in visible places, refer back to them every teachable moment you get, engraining them in your players' hearts and minds.

When our staff took over the program, we knew we had an undersized team that had just graduated a talented senior class. We had no feel for how many games we'd win or how good we could truly be. So we made up our mind—we're going to work harder, play harder, and give more effort than any team around, regardless of the score. We titled this mantra 5.1. The average play in a game of football lasts 5.0 seconds. But if we give just a little more effort—the 0.1—in all we do, we will succeed, in both life and football.

We talked about 5.1 all the time. We posted it on our goal board. We hung it on signs in the weight room and the locker room. We branded it everywhere we could—T-shirts, locker tags, playbooks, and even the practice field. We did our best to live it out, pushing our players to the limit in the weight room, putting in extra time preparing for games, and showing we cared about them off the field. We called out and rewarded 5.1 behaviors in our players to reinforce their achievements.

Over time, we heard players talking about 5.1 to push each other. We saw them living it out in the hallways and classrooms at school. We saw them learning to practice and play with the 5.1 effort we were asking of them. They were getting the message.

I have no idea if the Rule of Seven is a truly valid phenomenon—but I believe in it. It seems to apply in sports, academics, business, politics, and more. My personal experiences point to its truth. I do not know of compelling evidence for it, but I do know that persistence overcomes resistance.

If we are going to be men and women who make a lasting impact for Christ in the lives of others, we must realize that changing lives is a slow and challenging process.

If something is important, you must keep saying it. And when you think you've said it enough, keep saying it some more!

John the Baptist's persistence literally pointed numerous people to Jesus—even his own loyal followers. The end of John chapter 1 paints a picture of persistence that I've read over many times but failed to truly see and understand.

While leading his own disciples one day, John sees Jesus approaching and proclaims his holy identity.

"Look, the Lamb of God!"

He even testifies, putting his own credibility on the line, that based on what he has seen, Jesus is the very Son of God, "God's chosen one," the Messiah. John attests to the importance and majesty of Christ the King.

These are bold statements in a rousing and passionate call to action! But nothing happens.

I'm sure the disciples were listening. I'm sure he had their attentive ear. But change is slow.

Fast-forward twenty-four hours and John repeats the message: "Look, the Lamb of God!"

This time there was a different outcome.

"When the two disciples heard him say this, they followed Jesus."

What changed? Because he kept saying it, maybe John's persistence overcame resistance.

When John first said, "Look, the Lamb of God!" and introduced his disciples to the God of the Universe in human flesh, they just sat there and stared. How frustrating that must have been for John. But he wasn't dismayed. Instead, he kept the introduction going.

"Look, the Lamb of God!"

I hope you have a couple of people in your life whom you are trying to reach with the Gospel of Jesus Christ. If you don't, pray for God to identify a few individuals—friends, family, coworkers—and ask him to use you to introduce them to Jesus.

Once you have a few people picked to invest in, keep saying it. Understand that the Rule of Seven will likely be more like the Rule of Seven Hundred and Seventy-Seven! It's probably not going to happen in twenty-four hours as it did with John. You will likely have to keep praying, investing, showing, and saying, "Look, the Lamb of God!" over and over before there is action.

But keep saying it. Persistence overcomes resistance!

This week, keep investing in the lives of others. Stay the course. Don't be dismayed or frustrated. Change is slow. Let God work, and just keep saying it!

THIS WEEK, STRIVE...

☐ To identify a person or two with whom you will intentionally and purposefully share your faith. Start by coming before God in prayer, asking him in whom he wants you to invest. As you pray, contemplate individuals with whom you spend considerable amounts of time. Your established relationship will help open the door to share your beliefs freely.

☐ To plan the message you want to share with those God has placed on your heart. Pray for guidance and direction on what to say and to recognize the opportunity to say it. It could be as simple as sharing a difficult life experience and how God helped you overcome it, sharing something you learned at church, or it could involve asking the individual about past experiences, leading to conversation about what both of you believe.

☐ To keep saying it. Pray, persist, be patient. Don't give up. Let God move according to his plan and timing. If you continue to share and live out the Gospel for a watching world, they will see and hear, and when the time is right, many will believe!

You Keep What You Give Away
Week 26

One person gives freely, yet gains even more; another withholds unduly, but comes to poverty. A generous person will prosper; whoever refreshes others will be refreshed.

PROVERBS 11:24–25

Praise be to the God and Father of our Lord Jesus Christ, the Father of compassion and the God of all comfort, who comforts us in all our troubles, so that we can comfort those in any trouble with the comfort we ourselves have receive from God.

2 CORINTHIANS 1:3–4

Why does God give us any of the things we possess? Why does he allow us to have the life experiences through which we've lived?

He gives us tangible things we can touch, see, and feel: income and possessions we purchase with that income; children, spouses, and other family members; physical bodies with health, healing when we are sick or injured, and food and drink for nourishment. The list goes on.

He also gives us intangible things: comfort in grief or adversity; peace during uneasy times; confidence and assurance when we are afraid; courage and strength when we feel weak; and the ultimate intangible, unexplainable, unmerited gift—grace, made possible through the tangible death of Jesus on the cross.

Why does God allow us to possess and experience these things?

Some will say it's the reward for good works. Others will say it's karma—what goes around comes around. Another might say it's favor, and that these tangible and intangible things can be spoken into one's life.

All these reasons are completely wrong.

Why do we have what we have? Why have we experienced what we've experienced? Is it because we've earned our keep? Have we been through certain experiences because we are superior or deserving? Or because we've done something wrong? Does he give us these things to keep? Do we have these experiences to hold on to for ourselves?

None of the above.

All we have and everything we've been through is no accident. They are ours for a reason: so we can give them away.

It's essential to realize that everything we can see and experience is temporary—on loan from God for a short period of time. Psalm 24:1 says "The earth is the LORD's, and everything in it, the world, and all who live in it." Tangible, intangible, it's all his.

The key is this: We keep what we give away.

Consider when you learn something new and exciting. What do you instantly want to do? You want to tell somebody. Perhaps you even tell as many people as you can or will listen to you. You share this exciting new nugget of wisdom with them.

As you tell more and more people, it becomes more and more deeply engrained in you! Ask any teacher—one of the best ways to help a student learn is to have the student teach the material to someone else.

We keep what we give away.

Realize that there are people out in our world who have your name on them. In other words, no one can reach them for the sake of the Gospel but you. You have something—it could be financial resources, a leadership position of influence, a specific talent, a life experience or story—that no one else can offer but you.

My wife and I have undergone a combined fifteen surgeries due to athletic injuries, so it shouldn't come as a surprise that we've been blessed to be used by God to minister to injured athletes. We can encourage them, share our experiences, discuss their frustrations and disappointments, and give them hope through Jesus Christ.

Unless you're bionic like us from your athletic days, I doubt you can reach these athletes like we can. But I guarantee there is someone you can reach who my wife and I cannot. You might have financial or material resources you can give to meet needs. You may have a similar experience of grief so that you can offer comfort. You might have a similar personality or interest that can connect you with someone.

You are blessed to be a blessing. You have been comforted to give others comfort. And when you give away what God has given you, you are engraining in yourself a spirit of humble service, the spirit of Christ himself.

This week, give, serve, and love, remembering that **everything we possess is on loan to us for a short time.** The measure of our days is not in what we get, but rather in what we give away!

THIS WEEK, STRIVE...

- ☐ To reflect on an act of generosity you experienced. It could be something you did or something someone else did for you. What happened? What were the effects? What were the unseen outcomes? Did the kindness multiply?

- ☐ To consider something you have that could greatly impact others. Maybe you have a story of overcoming adversity you can share, or a room in your house that you can open up to others. Maybe you have extra clothing or shoes you can donate. Do you have a passion for teaching or coaching that you can use more? What can you give away?

- ☐ To set a goal for what you will share. Fully define what you will give away. When and where will you do it? Whom will you be impacting? Be specific. Then put it on your calendar, in your planner, on your phone, or write it where you will see it often. Make it happen and make a difference! You are blessed to be a blessing to others!

PULSE CHECK FRIEND
WEEK 27

One who has unreliable friends soon comes to ruin, but there is a friend who sticks closer than a brother.

PROVERBS 18:24

One of my dear friends and mentors likes to say (astutely, I might add) that there are two kinds of people in this world:

The majority, who are always saying "What can you do for me?"

And the minority, who are always saying "What can I do for you?"

I call the "What can I do for *you*?" people in my life pulse-check friends. They are constantly putting themselves and their agendas aside, and instead they take time to check my pulse to see how I am doing—mentally, physically, and spiritually. They ask questions like "How are you really doing? What's going through your head? What are you struggling with right now?"

I was reminded of these categories of people during a visit to Chicago that happened to fall on Father's Day weekend. As my wife and I walked down the sidewalk filled with retail-hungry people, a man caught my eye by the store where we were heading.

He was perched up, sitting on the brick ledge outside the large picture window of the storefront. His joyful smile never dissipated. He was holding the door for every customer entering and leaving the store. The man greeted each with a nod, smile, and a well wish for their day.

I have no idea what his story was. The cynic might say he was doing this to earn some tips. Maybe he was resting while his wife was on a shopping spree. (I've heard men do that at times. No personal experience.) Perhaps the store was paying him a bit to be a greeter. Who knows? But the point is this: He was a "What can I do for you?" person. A professional pulse checker.

Before I proceed, you need to know that my wife is a "What can I do for you?" person as well. She is, without question, one of the most selfless, others-centered people I have ever met. If there ever was a faithful servant, it is her. She checks a lot of pulses.

As we entered the store, the man greeted us with smiling enthusiasm, asking us how we were, and wishing us a great rest of our day. But the pulse checker had met his match in my wife. Stepping aside from the flow of people entering the store, my wife instead took a moment to ask him how he was doing and wished him a happy Father's Day.

"My goodness!" the man exclaimed. "Thank you very much. You know what? Hardly anyone has asked me how I'm doing, and you're the only person all day to wish me a happy Father's Day. So thank you!"

I found the man's response sorrowing. All that joy he was sharing with hundreds, maybe thousands of people who entered that store, and nothing in return.

I hope and pray that you are a pulse checker for others, a "What can I do for you?" person. But regardless of how much you are serving others, please know this: We all need a pulse-check friend.

It's pleasing to our Lord when we continuously serve him and others. In fact, we are commanded to do this (see Matthew 25:34–46). It is what God desires of us. But on our own, we do not possess the strength to serve unless we have two things:

1. PULSE CHECKERS AROUND US. ("One who has unreliable friends soon comes to ruin.")

We all *must* have four to five key pulse-check friends who are looking out for us and asking the hard questions. God designed us for quality companionship and community. The strength is in the pack, not in the lone wolf.

2. A RELATIONSHIP WITH THE ULTIMATE PULSE CHECKER. ("There is a friend who sticks closer than a brother.")

Jesus Christ, the Lamb of God, is the ultimate pulse-check friend. He is the "friend who sticks closer than a brother." His actions proved it when he laid down everything to come to earth, dwell among us, and then die for us. Come to him early and often. He desires to help carry your joys and struggles.

This week, I challenge you to two things:

1. CHANGE YOUR VOCABULARY TO THAT OF A PULSE CHECKER.

I'd like to let you in on something I've been working on. Every time someone calls me, or anytime someone enters my office— even if it's an interruptive hassle—I've been working on training myself to say, "What can I do for you?" I'm not there yet, but I've found it helps me set my mind on meeting the needs of the other person, and more often than not, it also puts me in a position to be a pulse-check friend to others where they are struggling or in need.

2. DEVELOP YOUR PULSE-CHECK LIST.

Write down, store in your phone, add to your e-mail address book—whatever works for you—a list of five pulse-check friends. I'll give you number one on the list—Jesus. Only four more to go! You probably already have this list informally in your mind, but take a moment to consider the quality friends in your life. You'll need them as you live and serve for Jesus each day.

Let's all be "What can I do for you?" pulse checkers each day as we display Jesus to a watching world!

THIS WEEK, STRIVE…

- ☐ To identify your pulse-check friend list. Write down, store in your phone, or create a contact group in your e-mail with the four or five people who will pick up the phone or come see you anytime, anywhere, for anything you need.
- ☐ To formally invite those on your list to be your pulse checkers. You may informally call these people when you need something,

and they may reach out to you to check your pulse. But make it official. Give them permission to check your pulse and offer the same in return.

☐ To use more pulse-checker vocabulary each day. When you answer the phone, look to ask the question, "What can I do for you?" When you talk to others, ask "How can I help?" Don't be shy about asking "How are you doing?" Start building habits that put you in the mind-set of serving others daily!

MICROMANAGEMENT
WEEK 28

Moses took his seat to serve as judge for the people, and they stood around him from morning till evening. When his father-in-law saw all that Moses was doing for the people, he said, "What is this you are doing for the people? Why do you alone sit as judge, while all these people stand around you from morning till evening?"… "What you are doing is not good. You and these people who come to you will only wear yourselves out. The work is too heavy for you; you cannot handle it alone."

EXODUS 18:13–18

From the day I could say *football*, I wanted to play quarterback. I played the position from the day organized football began in third grade to the day my playing career ended.

I've always loved being in command of the huddle. I've always embraced the expectation of delivering when the game is on the line. I cherished the responsibility to care for, inspire, and challenge teammates. I engrossed myself in the study of the game, the scheming, and the preparation. I relished being able to call the game at the line of scrimmage and manipulate the defense for the benefit on our team.

But as I reflect on my years in the game and, in particular, why I love the quarterback position, I've come to a rather startling realization. A realization that is a little embarrassing to admit.

I love control.

Perhaps you do too.

There's a certain element of power to it. You feel in command. You're the leader of the pack. You know (or think you know) what the future holds and what is best. You feel on top of things, at peace, and at ease. You have certainty, clarity, and direction. You are in charge, and you feel good. But I've got news for all of us.

We're not in control or in charge. And if we're not careful, our need for control can lead to something very unhealthy and counterproductive: micromanagement.

I would define *micromanagement* as trying to be all things to all people. It's getting caught up in details that are not yours to get caught up in. It's doing things that are not yours to do. It's overstepping boundaries.

Now there are times in life when you must micromanage. Parenting is an example. A young son or daughter simply cannot manage his or her own life. In essence, as a parent, you are keeping that child alive and on the right path! If your young son says, "May I go out and play?" you will likely respond by micromanaging. "Yes, you may play for thirty minutes until dinner is ready. But only with these toys and only in the backyard where I can see you."

But if your son is now a young adult, away at college, and he calls home and says, "May I go out and play?" you (hopefully) won't respond by micromanaging! You will likely respond by asking, "Is this a joke?" You don't know his homework load, what's on his calendar, or what his friends are doing. You simply cannot micromanage him.

Sadly, I've seen parents who want that type of control over their children even as they become young adults.

But God isn't one of them. God is our heavenly parent. But he doesn't micromanage us. Nor does he want us to micromanage. He wants us to trust in him and in other people.

One of God's greatest leaders of all time—Moses, who led Israel out of Egypt—was a micromanager. Yes, in his defense, the Israelites did often act like spiritual five-year-olds. But Moses allowed himself to fall into the trap of control and micromanagement of the people's lives. He sat alone as judge, and from sunup to sundown people came to him with disputes, which he would prayerfully resolve. His father-in-law, Jethro, came along and made a simple yet profound observation: "What you are doing is not good" (Exodus 18:17).

As we look closer at Exodus 18, this account of Moses as Israel's judge offers us three practical points that we can apply to our lives and leadership roles at home, at work, at church, and in the community:

1. MICROMANAGING IS COUNTERPRODUCTIVE. ("They stood around him from morning till evening" [v. 13].)

People were wasting time waiting for Moses to decide for them, when they could be working on their own problem-resolution skills! When we micromanage other people's lives, we waste valuable time and hinder their development.

2. MICROMANAGING IS TOO HEAVY. ("Whenever they have a dispute, it is brought to me, and I decide" [v. 16].)

Moses was carrying the weight of the world on his shoulders. Everyone's drama rested in his hands. When we micromanage, we carry baggage that is not ours to carry.

3. MICROMANAGING IS TIRING. ("You and these people who come to you will only wear yourselves out" [v. 18].)

Moses had to be exhausted after listening to everyone's problems all day, every day. So too, when we micromanage what is not ours to decide, we create undue fatigue and unrest in our lives.

This week, we're all bound to have an opportunity or temptation to micromanage. Instead, ask God for his help to lead well and to trust. Replace worry and desiring control with faith in God and others. The results might be different than you would have preferred, but with God's help, it will be a better journey along the way!

THIS WEEK, STRIVE…

☐ To tell someone you trust the one thing that wears you out, the burden that drains you of joy, energy, or time. Is it an area you are micromanaging? Is it something or someone you care about, so letting go is a struggle? Are you failing to trust? Talk through ways you can release this burden by turning it over to God.

☐ To do a quick calendar evaluation. Look at your schedule this week, specifically searching for non-essential tasks. Do you really need to do them? Do you really need to be involved? Why are they on your calendar? Is it a micromanagement, control, or trust issue? This week remove from your plate one item that can be trusted to others. How did this feel? What was the outcome?

☐ To use worry, fear, or distrust as a cue to pray. Each time you feel uneasy, come before God. When you start worrying or doubting, consider it a trigger to pray. It can be a quick, silent, one-sentence prayer asking for God's help. What difference do you notice?

WHAT WE CAN'T SEE
WEEK 29

For I know the plans I have for you," declares the LORD, "plans to prosper you and not to harm you, plans to give you hope and a future.

JEREMIAH 29:11

When disappointment strikes, when failures happen, when trials arise, when you suffer great loss, have you ever considered what God might be *saving* you from?

What if our deepest disappointments are blessings in disguise, if seemingly unanswered prayers are really God's mercies, if getting what we think we want is really the worst thing for us?

These are questions I've pondered over and over since I suffered a great disappointment in my life—being released by a franchise in the National Football League. Leading up to and during my time in the NFL, there was absolutely no doubt in my mind that professional football was going to be my career path for at least a few years. I had dreamed of that moment for years and worked tirelessly toward achieving my goal. I felt prepared, ready, and confident. Other options never even entered my mind. There was no plan B. Football was simply what I was going to do.

Or so I thought!

Throughout the Bible, we often see that for some people, getting what they want is actually the worst thing for them. We read multiple examples of God giving people over to their desires (see Job 8:4, Psalm 78:50, Psalm 81:12, Acts 7:42, and Romans 1:24–28) because they will not submit to his will for their lives. Each time, the story ends in destruction.

Or consider Jesus' disciples and their struggle to grasp that he was going to be crucified and rise from the dead (see Matthew 16:21–23). When Jesus died on the cross, his disciples must have thought, "This is the worst thing that could ever happen!" But the reality is, they were witnessing the *greatest* thing God ever did!

For me, perhaps an NFL career would've been detrimental to my marriage. The rigors of the schedule and lifestyle might have pulled me away from God. I could have suffered a debilitating injury. Maybe I am simply more useful to God and can make a difference in others' lives as an employee, coach, and a leader in other capacities, rather than as a player.

Have you reflected on these types of questions in your own life? Have you considered that some of your greatest heartaches and hardships might actually be the best things that ever happened to you in the long run?

For now, all we can do is speculate. We only see part of God's plan. Someday, when we see him face-to-face, it will all make perfect sense. We'll see all the connections, all the reasons, and all God's perfect purposes for everything he flawlessly laid before us in this life. "For now we see only a reflection as in a mirror; then we shall see face to face. Now I know in part; then I shall know fully, even as I am fully known" (1 Corinthians 13:12).

But I do know this: the longer we walk with the Lord, the more we realize how trustworthy he is. This week, take comfort in God's perfect design for your life journey. Thank him for what he's doing each day, even if you aren't entirely sure what he's up to yet. He "knows the plans" he has in store for you, and they are entirely in your best interests—filled with hope and a bright future—for our good and his glory!

THIS WEEK, STRIVE...

- ☐ To spend a little time this week reflecting on a difficult or adverse circumstance that you've overcome in your life. Has it worked out for good in the end? How has God used this circumstance in a positive way—either for you or for others? Do you trust him more now as a result of this challenge?
- ☐ To commit Jeremiah 29:11 to memory this week. What speaks to you? What about this verse brings you comfort and peace? Write it down.

☐ To write down at least three ways you plan to use the words and message of Jeremiah 29:11 moving forward. Will you share it with someone else to help them through a difficult time? Will it strengthen your ability to trust God? Will it cause you to more readily obey his will for your life?

FAMILY MATTERS?
WEEK 30

Now the overseer is to be above reproach, faithful to his wife, temper-
ate, self-controlled, respectable, hospitable, able to teach, not given to
drunkenness, not violent but gentle, not quarrelsome, not a lover of
money. He must manage his own family well and see that his children
obey him, and he must do so in a manner worthy of full respect. (If
anyone does not know how to manage his own family, how can he
take care of God's church?) …A deacon must be faithful to his wife
and must manage his children and his household well.

1 TIMOTHY 3:2–12

How do you measure trust?

It's a tough question to answer, isn't it? After all, trust isn't exactly
quantifiable. Some might measure trust through people's words—what
they say and how they say it. Some might measure trust by behavior and
how a person treats others or handles certain situations. Yet others might
base trust on actions and whether an individual gets the job done in the
appropriate manner.

As I've gotten older, more experienced, and (I hope) a little wiser,
I've come to measure trust with a new metric: how a person manages his
or her family.

If I'm able to spend some time around a person with his or her
spouse and kids, I can catch a tell-all glimpse into how well that person
treats others, gets a job done, and carries out daily business. I've come
to learn that household management is an excellent metric of trust.

But I've also come to a frightening realization: Based on the family
management metric, the world is becoming less and less trustworthy.

The US Census Bureau's latest birth and family study results will
knock your socks off:

- Thirty-six percent of all children in the United States are born to unmarried "partners."
- Births to unmarried women increased 80 percent from 1980 to 2007 (a 20 percent increase from 2002 to 2007 alone!).
- Forty percent of all children born in the United States will be living in a cohabitating (unmarried couples living together) household by age twelve. This number is growing.
- Forty percent of all US children will see their parents split up by age fifteen. [1]

As the Apostle Paul outlines the characteristics of successful church leaders in 1 Timothy 3, he poses a rhetorical question with laser-like accuracy: "If anyone does not know how to manage his own family, how can he take care of God's church?"

Managing one's own family has implications everywhere. Research clearly outlines the negative effects of unmarried cohabitating parents and single-parent households on the family unit and on children. These include poor developmental outcomes, lack of stability, less educational advancement, less economic freedom, and children who are more likely to have their own failed marriages. But consider the much broader ripples and ramifications of this trend. If more than one-third of our nation cannot manage a household and hold family in the sacred regard God desires the family to be held in:

- How can business be managed in the marketplace?
- How can children be taught in our educational system?
- How can patients be cared for in our hospitals?
- How can citizens be represented well in our government?

If we cannot manage the most important blessing God has entrusted to us—family—how can we manage anything else? Can we be trusted with other things?

I'm not sure we can.

What's the best first step toward remedying this dangerous breakdown of the family unit in our nation? It's a matter of priority.

Worshippers in Jesus' time offered sacrifices to God at the temple for various reasons—to atone for sin, to express thanksgiving, to show fellowship, to represent peace. God's command was that all sacrifices be holy and perfect, without blemish. But even when a worshipper brought his best to the altar, Jesus issued the following command:

> If you are offering your gift at the altar and there remember that your brother or sister has something against you, leave your gift there in front of the altar. First go and be reconciled to them; then come and offer your gift. (Matthew 5:23–24)

In other words, give your best at home first. Then, Jesus says, give your best to me. How do we apply this?

If you have an issue at work, at church, in the community, or anywhere other than home, be sure to settle things at home first. If you're going to use your gifts and talents at work, in the community, at church, or anywhere outside the home, that's great. Just be sure to use your gifts at home first.

Show me a great parent, and I'll show you someone who can be a great business leader. Show me a committed parent, and I'll show you someone who can be an outstanding nurse. Show me a strong household leader, and I'll show you someone you can trust.

Today, consider the blessing and responsibility of leading your family. It's a high calling. "From everyone who has been given much, much will be demanded" (Luke 12:48). But God values it greatly. If you desire to succeed in your daily endeavors, are you succeeding at home first? Let's be men and women God can trust, starting with his primary gift to— our families.

THIS WEEK, STRIVE...

☐ To make a list of the ways you measure trust. What are key trust indicators for you? Is it how someone speaks? Is it actions? Is it production? Is it how someone manages his or her personal life?

What matters to you when it comes to trust?

☐ To analyze your trust list in light of your own life. Do you show your trustworthiness in the same ways that you measure it in others? Is there any misalignment? What changes might you consider making?

☐ To pay special attention to your interactions with your family. How are you relationships with them? Are you home enough? Are your priorities in order? Is the way you handle one of God's most precious gifts proving you are trustworthy?

FAKE FAITH?
WEEK 31

But our citizenship is in heaven. And we eagerly await a Savior from there, the Lord Jesus Christ, who, by the power that enables him to bring everything under his control, will transform our lowly bodies so that they will be like his glorious body.

PHILIPPIANS 3:20–21

Nothing reunites family quite like a wedding.

My friend found himself together again with family members from around the world as his sister said her marriage vows. Given the global nature of his family, the wedding celebration brought together the many unique cultures, opinions, preferences, and viewpoints of his aunts, uncles, and cousins, and this included faith and theology.

As the celebration weekend progressed, my friend had the opportunity to discuss spirituality in greater detail with some of his family members. My friend is a Christ follower. Much of his family is Muslim.

They discussed many aspects of faith over dinner, but the most interesting discourse centered on the subjects of life and death. Someone made a rather shocking statement at the table: "Christianity is a fake faith."

Naturally, my friend came to the defense of his Lord and Savior. But the issue wasn't Christ. It was Christians.

In the Islamic faith, my friend's family members explained that they believe deeply in the cycle of life and in allowing Allah's plans to be carried to fruition. So when it comes to life and death, if someone dies, of course there is grief. It's only natural. But no one gets upset, no one blames Allah, no one allows themselves to be deeply shaken. It's all a matter of trust.

But in their observations over the years, my friend's family members explained that they've seen many so-called Christians at a loss with death. They've seen Christians get angry. They've seen Christians give up on living life. They've seen Christians become hostile, blaming God, and turning their backs on the source of their faith.

In their minds, by these types of reactions, Christianity seems like shifting sand at best.

Fake faith.

As I listened to my friend recount these conversations, all I could think was, that's a really good point.

The true test of faith is a moment of hitting rock bottom in one's life. When things don't go as planned, we lose something of value or someone dear to us, and life itself seems to be crumbling and caving in.

How one responds in these dire circumstances says a lot about one's faith and the strength of one's beliefs.

There's no greater dire circumstance than the death of a loved one. But in that moment, as followers of Jesus—the One who died that we might live—do we truly believe the words of Paul? "But our citizenship is in heaven. And we eagerly await a Savior from there, the Lord Jesus Christ, who, by the power that enables him to bring everything under his control, will transform our lowly bodies so that they will be like his glorious body" (Philippians 3:20–21).

Are we living in a manner that shows we truly believe this world is not our home? Though we grieve the loss of life, do we also celebrate with expectation the eternal life that is to come? Do we *truly believe* the core of our faith—that Jesus Christ rose from the dead, and in so doing, opened the path for us to one day rise to eternal life with him?

Clearly, from the perspective of my friend's family, as a body of Christ, we've still got some work to do.

This week, when things are at their worst, let's be at our spiritual best. Let's erase all doubts of a fake faith. Let's be living examples of a real faith that isn't shaken, even by death, but that instead eagerly awaits citizenship in Heaven through our Lord Jesus Christ. May our witness before a watching world show that our faith in Jesus is the real deal!

THIS WEEK, STRIVE...

☐ To monitor your reactions when you don't get your way. What happens? Do you get angry? Do you say things you shouldn't? Does it ruin your day? How is your attitude? Do you blame God? What does your reaction say to those watching you?

☐ To set aside five minutes simply to think about Paul's statement, "Our citizenship is in heaven." Five minutes uninterrupted— no phone, no e-mail, no TV, no distractions. Just dwell on this truth. What does it mean to you? Where is your focus? Is it on the worldly concerns of everyday life? Or is it on how those concerns fit into a much broader plan for your life—both now, and, if you know Jesus, for eternity? How can you begin to shift your citizenship to where it belongs?

☐ To pray for God's direction about how you can be a more effective example of faith in Jesus to a watching world. What is one practical action you can take this week?

THE NOISE IN OUR HEADS
WEEK 32

"Woe to the obstinate children," declares the LORD, *"to those who carry out plans that are not mine, forming an alliance, but not by my Spirit, heaping sin upon sin;" … This is what the Sovereign* LORD, *the Holy One of Israel, says: "In repentance and rest is your salvation, in quietness and trust is your strength, but you would have none of it."*

ISAIAH 30:1, 15

James Junior, age one, shifted his gaze from the matchbox car on my kitchen floor toward the electrical outlet nearby. Junior's eyes locked on the wall plug as if the electrical outlet had engaged some form of magnetic, hypnotic force field on him. The little boy rose to his feet and began wobbly lumbering toward the outlet, a drooling smile on his face.

Before I resume the story, a little context: "Junior" is the son of a former college teammate of mine. His dad, James Senior, was the right tackle on our offensive line during my playing career. James grew up in the heart of Detroit, Michigan. He stands six foot four and is the most trim 330-pound man you'll ever see. Dreadlocks flow down his back and tattoos adorn his arms. As a player, James was intense and relentless. I have seen him plant defensive ends so deep in the turf that they began growing flowers. And since I played quarterback, believe me when I say that James has literally preserved my life from angry, blitzing linebackers on multiple occasions. James is a great bodyguard, and an even better friend.

Despite his ferocious play on the field, away from the game James is a gentleman with a magnetic personality and a gracious heart. But you can now begin to understand how his physical stature and presence would be quite intimidating and imposing to a stranger. You can also begin to understand that Junior is much larger than the average one-year-old!

Back to the action. Junior's wobbly walk toward the electrical outlet turned into a top-heavy trot that was slowly gaining momentum. Junior extended his right arm before him, his pudgy right index finger pointing at the intriguing outlet. His smile turned to laughter, producing a couple of drool bubbles as he gleefully approached the wall plug he desired to touch and investigate.

It had now become clear that Junior was not to be denied his first encounter with electricity. As I sprung from my chair to intercept the bobbling baby boy from electrocuting himself, a loud sound reverberated throughout my whole house.

"Hey!" a deep baritone voice bellowed. It was my six-foot-four, 330-pound friend James.

Immediately, Junior went dead in his tracks, stopping instantly on a dime. The little boy appeared to turn to stone. After a moment of complete stillness, Junior slowly and cautiously turned his head to peer over his shoulder at his dad, a blank expression on his face.

"No," James said to his young son.

Without hesitation Junior turned around, walked a few steps, heavily plopped back on my kitchen floor, and once again began to vigorously drive his matchbox car around in circles.

Stunned and also impressed by the unfolding of these events, I sat back in my chair to resume my conversation with James. As I did so, my wife made the million-dollar observation:

"He recognizes his daddy's voice."

Do you recognize your Heavenly Daddy's voice?

If I'm brutally honest with myself, I'm afraid I often have to answer that question with a no. As painful as that is for me to admit, I bet you find yourself in the same boat from time to time too.

There's a lot of noise in our heads, and it makes our Heavenly Daddy's voice hard to recognize. Like Junior, we are running toward danger, but, unlike Junior, we cannot hear or recognize the voice of ultimate truth.

Our to-do lists are long. At work we have appointments to keep, deadlines to meet, and people are counting on us. Our spouses need our love and support. We have children to invest in and raise and friends who are important to us. We have church and community commitments to which we are passionate about devoting time and resources. We enjoy hobbies and recreation. We desire to be healthy, so we commit time to fitness and being physically active.

Somewhere in that myriad of activity, rather than above the busyness where it belongs, our relationship with God competes with the noise in our heads. We attempt to pray but our mind drifts to work. We sit to read God's word, but our thoughts move to the massive number of e-mails in our inbox. We intend to join a group Bible study, but other commitments win out instead. We listen to a sermon on podcast while driving, and then get out of the car only to realize we can't remember a single word. We hope to end our day with quiet time before the Lord, but find ourselves waking up to the chiming of our morning alarm, realizing we fell asleep mid-prayer.

Of all these I am guilty culprit number one! But God has seen this pattern that slowly pushes him away. Frankly, it is like Junior running to stick a finger in an electrical outlet: it is sheer danger. Our Heavenly Daddy speaks strongly and sternly against it through his prophet Isaiah, as he addresses the nation of Israel: "Woe to the obstinate children," declares the LORD, "to those who carry out plans that are not mine, forming an alliance, but not by my Spirit, heaping sin upon sin" (Isaiah 30:1).

Obstinate means fixed, stubborn, set in one's ways, immoveable. We are running toward the wall outlet, about to get shocked, but we won't change. There's too much noise in our heads pushing God out, but the growing volume of it continues to draw our attention astray. We "carry out plans" without seeking God first, we don't live by the Spirit, and we fall into sin.

What must we do? How do we turn down the noise and get back to recognizing our daddy's voice?

Later in chapter 30, Isaiah lays out two simple steps to turn down the noise in our lives: "This is what the Sovereign LORD, the Holy One of Israel, says: 'In repentance and rest is your salvation, in quietness and trust is your strength, but you would have none of it'" (v. 30).

1. Repent

It starts with owning the issue. If we feel far from God, chances are he hasn't moved; it's you and I who have strayed, chasing the noise in our heads. Admit it to him. Own your distraction. Ask for his forgiveness, patience, and help to make the necessary changes in your life.

2. Find solitude

Isaiah says it is in "rest" and "quietness" that we can find "salvation" and "strength." Make a relentless commitment to protecting uninhibited, undistracted time in prayer and God's word each day. Battle for it. Guard it at all costs. Find a way. Does it mean turning off your phone? Does it mean getting up earlier? Does it mean driving your car to the grocery store, parking in a distant corner of the lot, and doing devotions there? Get creative. But do whatever it takes.

Remember: It is impossible to recognize someone's voice without spending time with him.

Today, stop running toward the wall outlet and the danger of being far from God. Let's turn down the noise in our heads. Together, let's recognize our Heavenly Daddy's voice again, and let's follow his direction for our lives!

This week, Strive...

☐ To eliminate one source of excess noise in your life this week. Do you need to turn your cell phone off for a while, take a night off from watching television, or a break from social media? Tell someone you trust what noise you are going to eliminate and ask him or her to hold you accountable to your commitment.

☐ To consider how well you recognize God's voice in your life. Would you say you allow him to speak to you through his word?

Is your prayer life healthy? Are you in Christian fellowship with others through whom he can speak into your life? What do you need to consider changing?

☐ To replace the noise you eliminate with time in God's presence. This could mean extra time studying his word, in prayer, or reflecting and journaling about what God's doing in your life. How did it go? Were you able to sustain this new discipline all week? Could it become routine for you?

THE EXCHANGE
WEEK 33

And the things you have heard me say in the presence of many witnesses entrust to reliable people who will also be qualified to teach others.

2 TIMOTHY 2:2

My favorite event of the track-and-field portion of the Summer Olympics is the 4 x 100-meter relay. Why? Because anything can happen.

The fastest team coming into the finals doesn't always win, nor does the team favored by the media prognosticators. The qualifying times leading up to the main event can be thrown out the window. The race always comes down to one key element of the relay: the exchange.

Growing up, track and field was one of my favorite sports. Each year in our small community of Orrville, Ohio, my friends and I participated in our local Smith Dairy track meet—a day-long track-and-field competition for elementary school athletes, sponsored by a local business.

Every year I recruited three of my friends to be a part of the meet's 4 x 100-meter relay. Then my dad would get us together a couple times a week, starting about six weeks before the big day. We would gather at the local high school track with our relay baton, ready to practice for the upcoming race.

We were typically never the fastest team. We usually weren't the best team. But we won the race almost every year. Why? We had the best exchanges, the best baton passes.

When we practiced as a team, we didn't work on our starts from the blocks, or trying to run faster, or with better technical form. We focused on one thing and one thing only: the exchange.

There are three exchanges between each leg of the 4 x 100-meter race. Each exchange must occur in an exchange zone 20 meters long, with a 10-meter acceleration zone preceding it, allowing the next runner to gain speed before receiving the baton. Each relay team must pass the baton from one runner to the next within the exchange zone. Failure to pass the baton in the legal zone results in disqualification.

At the Olympic level, the exchange from one runner to the next has cost the US relay teams dearly over the last decade. In 2004, a poor exchange disqualified the women's team from what seemed like a sure gold medal. In 2008, the men's team suffered the same disappointing fate—missing the medal stand due to a butchered exchange.[1]

The exchange determines the outcome of the race. In similar fashion, the exchange of life determines the passing on of our faith.

We are all in the race of our lives, and right now is our time to pass the baton. The exchange is the dash that will be on our headstones at the cemetery someday. For example, mine will read: 1986–???

The number of years we live—represented by the dash and known only by God—this is our time to make the exchange. It's the figurative 20 meters of track that we have to pass the baton of our faith to as many people as possible before we're disqualified from this life.

Paul's command to Timothy about the exchange is undeniably clear. We are to take all we've learned about Jesus from our relationship with him and the faith in which we believe and "entrust" it "to reliable people who will also be qualified to teach others."

Passing the baton. For the Christ follower, it's not optional. It's the only way our faith in Christ lives on.

I'm not sure where you are in your life's race. Perhaps you just took your first steps into it, are in the middle, or maybe you're only a few steps away from crossing the finish line. In reality, it doesn't matter where you are in your journey. If there's breath in your lungs, you've still got time to make the exchange. So take on the challenge God places before us to pass the baton.

This week, pray and seek God's counsel. Who is awaiting the baton at the other end of your exchange? Who needs to hear the life-changing news of the Gospel from you right now?

The race is short; share your faith today!

THIS WEEK, STRIVE...

☐ To list three things you would want others to say of you at your funeral. What will be in your eulogy? What will your obituary say? Put another way, for what do you want to live your life? Capture it on paper.

☐ To assess your progress toward your desired life legacy. Are you in alignment and on track with what you hope to be remembered for? Will you get where you want to go? What must change to make your desired legacy reality?

☐ To set one goal or action item for change to better propel you toward your desired life legacy. Time is not on our side as we move through our life's race. In whom do you need to invest? Where do you need to make a bigger impact? How can you multiply yourself even more? Don't wait! Start today!

STAY BY YOUR KING
WEEK 34

Now a troublemaker named Sheba son of Bikri, a Benjamite, happened to be there. He sounded the trumpet and shouted, "We have no share in David, no part in Jesse's son! Every man to his tent, Israel!" So all the men of Israel deserted David to follow Sheba son of Bikri. But the men of Judah stayed by their king all the way from the Jordan to Jerusalem.

2 SAMUEL 20:1–2

Late one morning in the spring of my first year as a head football coach, I had just finished a meeting when my phone rang. It's a phone call I'll not soon forget. It was the lead teacher from our alternative school program. A young man I'd been mentoring was going to jail.

I'd developed a strong relationship with this student through coaching football. He was entering his senior season when I was hired, but academic eligibility issues kept him from playing on the team. So in an effort to get him on track to graduate, we enrolled him in our alternative school program, giving him the opportunity to recover credits while working at his own pace.

During this time I began meeting with him regularly, and he continued to participate in our off-season workouts to stay in shape. We discussed his goals and plans for the future, and we worked together to keep a laser focus on finishing high school well.

Things were going nicely until the young man made a poor choice late that winter. There were consequences from the school, and legal action was possible though unclear at the time. Despite this setback, we kept meeting weekly to discuss ways to overcome it and to stay on track for graduation.

As time progressed, he was charged and went to trial. Then I received this dreaded phone call. I quickly called his mom to gather more details, then I called a friend of mine who is a detective with the local police.

Two hours later, I found myself at the county prison with the young man's family. In the weeks that followed, my detective friend was able to help me visit the young man on multiple occasions until he was sent to another facility two hours away for the remainder of his sentence. I was able to visit him at the new location on a few occasions, and I joined with a group of other teachers and coaches who wrote to him regularly to provide encouragement. We wanted to ensure that not a week went by without a visitor or a piece of mail to read.

Why all this effort? I learned through this experience that prison can simplify a life. In many ways, prison strips away the complexities, stresses, and confusion inmates faced before their incarceration. The men are left with more focus and clarity than before they went to jail.

But often, this newfound clarity reveals something painful to prisoners: who their real friends are.

When you're behind bars, it doesn't take a genius to discover your loyal friends, to figure out who really cares about you. They're the ones who visit and write you regularly. They are there for you no matter what, and often there aren't many such friends.

Adversity reveals real friends who will stay by you regardless of circumstance.

King David knew the solitude of adversity well. During the later stages of his forty-year reign over Israel, Absalom, David's greedy, power-hungry son, built up a following so he could overthrow his father's throne. With his son's militant mob of support bearing down, David had no choice but to flee his home with his key advisors and military leaders while a great number of citizens under his leadership turned their loyalties to Absalom.

After some crafty military strategy by David and his commanders, Absalom and his forces were exposed in battle and Absalom was killed, allowing David to return to his rightful place as king. Joy abounded throughout the land! The king is back! Right?

Wrong. The peoples' loyalty was split between David and Absalom.

On top of the division, a naysayer and "troublemaker" named Sheba incited more adversity and difficulty: "We have no share in David, no part in Jesse's son! Every man to his tent, Israel!"

All the people abandoned David except the men of Judah, who "stay by their king," remaining loyal to David's reign.

You know what this feels like, don't you? A tough leadership decision at work leaves you feeling unsupported and even questioned by your coworkers. The medical course of action you deem best for your patient isn't well received by the rest of the care team. Your plan to help a student isn't embraced by his or her parents. Your open honesty with your manager ends up getting you burned in the end. Your difficult discussion with a friend about the dangerous path he or she is on ends up terminating the relationship altogether.

When you're in the throes of a trial, it doesn't take a genius to discover your loyal friends. They're the ones who visit. They are there for you no matter what, and often there aren't many such friends.

There is another king, in addition to David, who knows the loneliness of adversity we all experience in our lives: King Jesus. Rejected by his own people, scorned by the very ones he came to save, constantly under attack from the Pharisees, betrayed by a disciple he had trained and invested in for years. Arrested. Beaten. Mocked. Killed.

Jesus himself told his disciples: "Everyone will hate you because of me" (Mark 13:13). In other words: "Following me will reveal who your true friends are."

When we face the loneliness of adversity, Jesus too knows what it is to be abandoned in the midst of affliction.

Thus, he will never abandon us (see Deuteronomy 31:6).

This week, boldly do the right thing, no matter the cost of desertion, rejection, or unpopularity. Follow the lead of the loyal men of Judah and stay by your king—King Jesus—the one who will never abandon us!

This week, Strive...

- ☐ To consider one person in your daily life—family member, friend, coworker—with whom you disagree about something.

All points of contention aside, how are you responding to that person? Are you still showing them love and respect? Are you working to resolve the disagreement? Work hard this week to separate the person from the issue.

☐ To reflect on your prayer relationship with Jesus. Is it sporadic? Is it consistent? Do you come to him often? Do you only come to him when you need something? What needs to change?

☐ To spend time in prayer at least twice a day all week. Whether you feel you "need to" or not. If it helps, put a reminder note where you'll see it, set an alarm on your phone, or schedule it on your calendar. Be intentional about staying by your King Jesus. Build your relationship with him.

ALWAYS AMBASSADORS
WEEK 35

We are therefore Christ's ambassadors, as though God were making his appeal through us.

2 CORINTHIANS 5:20

One Saturday morning I needed to run some errands before starting my work around the house. As I decided which T-shirt to wear, I grabbed one I acquired several years ago through the Fellowship of Christian Athletes. The front read "JeSus" with the *S* largely capitalized in the shape of the famous, embossed, triangular Superman logo we've often seen across the chest of Clark Kent's caped uniform. The back of the shirt read "He's Already Saved The Day," with the FCA logo below.

As I made my final stop on the errand circuit—the grocery store—I found myself in one of the slowest moving checkout lines I've ever been in. Ever. The line slowly progressed over the course of about ten minutes. (Not an exaggeration here; I kept track!) Finally, I was second in line. I could see the light at the end of the tunnel.

Then an older couple in front of me began a full-blown conversation with the checkout clerk. It started with some friendly dialogue, but then turned into the couple asking numerous questions about the products they were purchasing, and then even progressed to sharing stories. The couple, though clearly very friendly, was completely oblivious to the growing line of customers behind them.

Admittedly, I'm an impatient person. But, in my own estimation, I was handling the checkout line congestion well so far—until the guy two parties behind made a comment directed at me about getting the line moving. Apparently, in his mind, I wasn't impatient enough!

The comment, coupled with my growing irritation about the wait, was like a trigger mechanism. I felt my brow get warm and sensed the sweat breaking on my forehead. My grip tensed a little bit as I tightened my fists. I grit my teeth back and forth, feeling the anger rising within me.

Then suddenly, and very thankfully, I remembered the shirt I was wearing, the one that said JeSus on the front. I took a deep breath, let the comment roll off my back, and as patiently as possible, allowed the older couple to finish their social hour with the checkout clerk.

As I drove home after my long wait in the grocery line, I began to think about what had just transpired minutes ago. I thought about what a hypocrite I would've been if I had lost my temper in public while wearing a JeSus T-shirt. I considered what a complete misrepresentation I would've been to what I dearly believe. Then I thought about a verse that I knew very well: "We are therefore Christ's ambassadors, as though God were making his appeal through us" (2 Corinthians 5:20).

As I reflected on these well-penned words, suddenly it hit me: I'm *always* wearing a JeSus shirt, every single day. And if you have experienced personal conversion to follow Jesus Christ, figuratively, you are too! We are "Christ's ambassadors."

In the political sense, an ambassador is an accredited diplomat sent by a country as its official representative to a foreign nation. I can't think of a better definition for who we are as servants of Jesus Christ our King. We are ambassadors—always.

He's won our hearts by grace. He has our loyalty. He's equipped and trained us with his word. We're prepared to go out into a foreign nation—the world. We've been sent by our Lord and Savior with his message—the Gospel of His loving grace.

Just like a nation's ambassador wears that nation's flag on his or her lapel, we are wearing the equivalent of a JeSus shirt every day. We are always his ambassadors.

What kind of job are you doing representing him?

Today, realize that if you are following Jesus, you're wearing his name across your chest every day! You are his ambassador. And this is a great responsibility not to be taken lightly. With every thought, word, and deed, may you live in such a manner that the God we represent can say: "Well done, good and faithful servant" (Matthew 25:21).

THIS WEEK, STRIVE...

☐ To make a list of all the people, places, and things for which you are an ambassador. List as many items as possible that you represent each day—family, your employer, church, other organizations, and more. Is the list longer than you anticipated?

☐ To prioritize the list in order from most important down to least important. Once arranged in priority order, write or type *GOD* at the top of the list in the header. Is he really there, at the top, in his rightful place? If not, who or what has been pushing him down your list?

☐ To review your list a minimum of three times this week. Scan the most important things for which you are an ambassador, starting with God. How are you doing? Can others tell what you represent by simply watching you and listening to you? Is your relationship with Christ apparent in and through the other items on your ambassador list? If not, where can you begin to make changes this week to live out what you believe?

THE RESPONSIBILITY OF FREEDOM
WEEK 36

You, my brothers and sisters, were called to be free. But do not use your freedom to indulge the flesh; rather, serve one another humbly in love. For the entire law is fulfilled in keeping this one command: "Love your neighbor as yourself."

GALATIANS 5:13–14

There's a way to tell if you appreciate the freedom we enjoy in the United States: How are you using it?

Not long ago, I was deeply stirred by the words of leadership expert Tim Elmore as he addressed the topic of freedom:

Anyone who enjoys the freedom of a car, a smart phone, name-brand clothes and some cash . . .without any responsibility with those freedoms will likely end up being a brat. Do you know anyone like that? Freedom minus responsibility equals entitlement. That doesn't make for a great country.... Today—I see too many people who want the perks of freedom without the price. It's time we pay for our freedom.[1]

If an "Amen" is appropriate here, I'll say it. "AMEN!"

Elmore is absolutely right. Freedom is not free. In the United States of America, our forefathers were visionary leaders who cast vision, communicated the direction, and led people toward a common goal. In response to their idealism and inspiration, military leaders strategized, mobilized united forces, and fought the battle for independence. Many people willingly and unselfishly gave their lives as the down payment for freedom that would one day become reality.

Enjoying that freedom without taking any responsibility for it leads to carelessness, recklessness, and narcissistic entitlement. Unfortunately, we're all seeing more and more of this in our nation with each passing year. We desire liberty and independence with no price. Free freedom.

The same is true in our spiritual lives. Like the freedoms we enjoy in our country, there is an incredible freedom—an eternal freedom—that is available to all of us. It is a freedom from our sin and the past, a release from all our mistakes, guilt, shame, and embarrassments. Paul goes so far to say in Galatians chapter 5 that we are "called to be free." In the spiritual sense, freedom is supposed to be a part of who we are in Christ Jesus. It is to be a part of our identity, engrained in our spiritual DNA, the core of our very being.

But there was a price for that eternal freedom. Though innocent, Christ was framed as a criminal and unfairly tried by the authorities. Beaten, insulted, mocked, and flogged to pieces. On the fringe of death before the crucifixion even began, he staggered as he carried his execution tool—the cross—toward Golgotha. Nailed at the hands and feet, raised to hang in the public eye, then pierced with a sword, he died a brutal death so we could be free.

Paul reminds us of this all-powerful question in our lives: You may be free in Jesus, but how are you using it?

"Do not use your freedom to indulge the flesh; rather, serve one another humbly in love. For the entire law is fulfilled in keeping this one command: "Love your neighbor as yourself."

This makes perfect sense because freedom doesn't work with irresponsibility. Responsible people don't need a plethora of laws, guidelines, and regulations. Integrity requires no rules. Responsible people take their freedom seriously and police themselves. Irresponsible people need laws and consequences at every turn. And unfortunately, every day there seems to be a new law or legislation being debated or passed by our political and civic leaders.

I'm afraid we're just not being very responsible for our freedom.

The Gospel of Christ demands more from us. God calls us to a higher standard, to be responsible for our spiritual freedom in Jesus. That calling is simple and to the point: one law, one command, one single rule of thumb. A perfect call to responsibility: "Love your neighbor as yourself."

Are you doing that? How are you using your freedom in Christ?

This week, enjoy your freedom. It is an incredible gift, not to be taken lightly. Be grateful, joyful, and humble. Not only do we live in the blessing of civil and political liberties, but we have the blessing of something far greater: the opportunity to have eternal freedom through the blood of Jesus.

Take responsibility for your freedom—by how you use it. Love others when they are unlovable. Serve others when they don't deserve it. Give generously until it hurts. Live sacrificially each day, expecting nothing in return.

Let's all be responsible for the gift of freedom we've received. It may be free to us, but Jesus paid an ultimate price for it. In return, may our lives be a living sacrifice of responsibility for Jesus!

THIS WEEK, STRIVE...

- [ ] To identify all areas of entitlement in your life. Consider the things you think you deserve, the things you think you have to have, and the things you take for granted. If it helps, make a list or discuss this with someone else. What is dangerous about this entitlement? What effect does it have on the way you live and act?
- [ ] To thank God each day this week for what you appreciate most about him. Is it his love? His grace? His provision? His peace? Be intentional about expressing your thanksgiving daily. Start each time of prayer by thanking him.
- [ ] To take responsibility for this gratitude toward God. He's given you the freedom to serve him with your specific gifts. How will you do that this week? Will you pray for someone in need? Will you support a ministry or mission? Will you spend time listening to someone going through a difficult time? Will you provide a meal? Find a way to sacrificially pay it forward out of your gratitude to God.

IS THIS ALL THERE IS?
WEEK 37

"Meaningless! Meaningless!" says the Teacher. "Utterly meaningless! Everything is meaningless." What do people gain from all their labors at which they toil under the sun? Generations come and generations go, but the earth remains forever.

ECCLESIASTES 1:2–4

During my time as a high school head football coach, colleges and universities across the country would bombard me each winter and spring with football camp literature. In a one batch of bulk mailings, the following statement caught my eye and I took a picture (for the sake of the head coach, I covered his name):

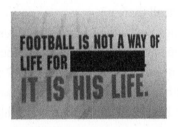

Football is his life? Is that all there is? Sure, I know it's just marketing propaganda to attract the next five-star recruit to his program—but seriously? Is that all that defines him?

To many boosters, fans, recruits, journalists, and our rabidly athletics-obsessed culture, the answer is yes. Coaching is the justification for his existence. His value lies in his ability to win football games. Sadly, throughout my time playing and coaching football, I have seen this all over the world of athletics.

One of my friends will tell you that, before following Jesus, he himself lived for the game of football. He was a walk-on who earned a scholarship after years of persistence and relentless hard work. During his third season in the program, he finally had the opportunity to be a defensive starter. It came on a big stage—against a Big 12 Conference, Bowl Championship Series opponent. It was what he had worked for and dreamed of for so long.

During a break on the bench between defensive series, my friend took a moment to survey the scene—it seemed to be all an athlete could ask for. But beyond the crowd, he found it to be just another football game, like so many he had played before.

"Is this all there is?" my friend wondered.

Consider the well-known movie *Chariots of Fire* and the famous line of British sprinter Harold Abrahams before competing in the 100-meter dash in the 1924 Paris Olympics: "I will raise my eyes and look down that corridor; four feet wide, with ten lonely seconds to justify my existence."

Abrahams went on to win the gold in the 100-meter. But was that truly the defining moment of his life? Was that ten-second sprint his reason for living? Is that all there is?

Finding meaning in the wrong things doesn't just happen in the athletic world: Find your value in your good looks? You'll gray and wrinkle. Find your security in your bank account or 401(k)? You can't take it with you. Find your worth in your possessions? They'll wear out, fade, or rust. Find refuge in your health? At some point, it will likely fail.

It's a hard reality, but one we must all face. On our own, this life is meaningless.

"Everything is meaningless," wrote King Solomon, the author of Ecclesiastes. Thousands and thousands of years from now, no one will remember what we owned, how much we earned, where we lived, or what we looked like. Except in rare cases, no one will even remember who we were.

What can give this meaningless life meaning? Something eternal.

The Gospel of John begins like this: "In the beginning was the word, and the word was with God, and the word was God" (John 1:1).

"The word" is translated from the Greek word *logos*. A sermon I recently heard explained that *logos* is likely better translated as "explanation" or "reason." In this context, the pastor explained, *logos* could mean "the reason for life."

In the beginning was the reason for life, and the reason for life was with God, and the reason for life was God.

Jesus is the reason for life, the One who gives meaning to the meaningless.

Jesus is our life. Not football, money, possessions, health, or other temporary things. He is the *logos*, the reason for life. He is everlasting. Are you living for him?

With Jesus, athletics becomes a platform to impact the lives of others; business can help share God's loving provision with the world; an investment account provides opportunity to bless those in need.

Thousands and thousands of years from now, those impacts, provisions, and blessings just might save a life for all eternity through the redeeming grace of Jesus Christ.

Today, remember that you don't need to justify your life on your own. Jesus "was delivered over to death for our sins and raised to life for our justification" (Romans 4:25). Our life and its meaning is found in him alone!

THIS WEEK, STRIVE...

☐ To evaluate the one thing you are pursuing more than anything else in your life. I'm sure you're busy and doing many things. But what's the one thing that is on your mind more than anything else? Work? Family? Finances? Your fitness or appearance? What occupies your thoughts?

☐ To consider why that one thing dominates your mind, time, and resources. Why are you pursuing it? Do you love it? Do you find identity and value in it? Are you afraid of losing it? Why are you chasing it? Is it worth chasing? What's your inner motivation?

☐ To turn over your top pursuit to God. Pray and ask him to align your life with his will. Dare to give him control, then see what he does and how he uses you. How much more meaning could your life and its pursuits have with him?

SHIFTING HIS GLANCE
WEEK 38

He went away a second time and prayed, "My Father, if it is not possible for this cup to be taken away unless I drink it, may your will be done."

MATTHEW 26:42

At a recent Fellowship of Christian Athletes study I attended, one of the students presented a great visual illustration:

He placed five empty cups numbered 1 through 5 on the table. He then read five scenarios of sin, ranging from cheating on an exam to murder. Then he asked the group to rank the sins from the worst to the most minor. The group decided scenario 4 was the most minor sin, so the student poured a small amount of red Hawaiian Punch in cup number 4. Then the group deemed scenario 5 was the gravest sin, so the student filled cup number 5 to the top with punch. At the end, each cup held a different amount of punch based on the group's perception of each sin.

The student then shared the punch line (some pun intended!) of the illustration. From our perspective, each cup appears to be filled to a different level. Each sin seems to carry a different weight. In our mind's eye, we view some sins as being worse than others. But from God's perspective, looking down on the cups, all he sees is that the cup is full. All he sees is our sin.

Left to our own devices, we tend to rationalize our actions. We justify our mistakes by looking around at the mistakes of others. We compare away our shortcomings and faults, dismissing them as "not as bad as what he did" or telling ourselves "at least I didn't do what she did." We look around to feel better about ourselves, but God looks down and sees our entire life before him—both the finest moments and the moments we'd rather forget.

The five cups of punch sat lifelessly on the table, serving as a reminder of the humble condition we are in on our own. But thankfully we are not on our own. We serve a God of grace who, in that grace, is willing to shift his glance from our sinful selves to the sinless Savior.

In the words of the renowned hymn, "Before the Throne of God Above":

> Because the sinless Savior died
> My sinful soul is counted free
> For God the just is satisfied
> To look on him and pardon me.

Jesus was humble enough to say "may your will be done" to the Father, and in so doing, he drank the cup you and I deserved. Our cup is empty and the burden is no longer ours' to bear.

When others look at us in this life, what do they see? They might view us as parents, friends, employees, coworkers, fellow church members, or family. They might view us as successes, failures, people they love, people who annoy them, people they trust, or people they want to avoid. They might view us for our accomplishments, our possessions, or our position in the community.

But what does God see?

I'm thankful that when God looks at us, he doesn't see us in the earthly light in which others see us. He doesn't see our cup filled with sin, faults, and shortcomings. In fact, I'm thankful that when God looks at us, he doesn't even see us; he sees Jesus, slain and risen to save us. The cup was not taken away from him, so that it could be taken away from us! Because of Jesus' sacrifice on the cross, God doesn't look at our sin, he looks at his son.

Today rejoice! Your cup is no longer counted full. God doesn't see your sin. He doesn't even see you. He sees Jesus.

Take time today (and every day) to thank God for this underserved gift of grace! Praise him that he is the God who shifts his glance!

THIS WEEK, STRIVE...

- ☐ To compare and contrast the way God views sin and the way we view sin. What's similar? What are major differences? Why do we tend to rank sins by their severity? Why do we tend to justify some actions, though we know they are wrong?
- ☐ To consider sin and its role in your life. Think about your thoughts, words, and deeds. How do you typically perceive yourself? As a good person? Or as someone in need of God's grace and forgiveness?
- ☐ To spend time in prayer each day this week purely focused on thanksgiving that Jesus died on the cross in our place, for our sin, and then rose from the dead. Do you understand the significance of this sacrifice? Do you fully appreciate what he's done for us?

KEEP YOUR TESTS TESTS
WEEK 39

Watch and pray so that you will not fall into temptation. The spirit is willing, but the flesh is weak.

MATTHEW 26:41

After the infamous Enron scandal blew up to mass proportion back in 2001, many business and media pundits thought we'd never see such greed or dishonesty ever again. But unfortunately, they were wrong. That hasn't been the case.

The US Securities and Exchange Commission brought fifty-eight insider-trading cases against 131 persons and organizations in 2012 alone.[1] In fact, from 2009 to 2012, the SEC has taken action on 168 insider-trading cases—more than in any other three-year time frame in the commission's history. These cases involved illegal profits totaling almost $600 million that executives, attorneys, and financial professionals made by trading with illicit, non-public information.[2]

What's the cause of this continued self-indulgence, dishonesty, and materialism? Some might say it's the economic recession. Others might say it's a lack of moral values. Others might say it's pressure to succeed financially. Still others might say it's just covetous greed.

But I think it's something different. It's a failure to keep tests tests.

A mentor and friend of mine taught me that the best way to avoid temptation is to keep your tests tests. Here's what that means:

It's all about the arm's-length principle. When we are faced with something "tempting" in life—like the enticement of financial wealth, the draw of vanity or physical attraction, the allure of power and status, or the pull of gossip and slander—we often call it a temptation. But that's not what it is truly is. That's the wrong terminology.

It is really a test. What are we going to do with this thing that has caught our eye? How are we going to respond to it? How will we act? What will we do next? That's a test. A test only becomes a temptation when we bring it within arm's length.

Consider a hug. When I keep something or someone away from me at arm's length, there's no embrace or acceptance. That's a test. But when I bring that something into my arms, holding it close, and beginning to clinch, grip, and squeeze it, now the test has become a temptation.

So we understand the difference between a test and a temptation. But how do we keep our tests tests? Jesus offers some insight in Matthew 26: **"Watch and pray so that you will not fall into temptation. The spirit is willing, but the flesh is weak."**

1. Watch and pray.

Be aware of the tests around you. You observe them all the time. You know where they lurk in your daily life. Pray for God's help. Don't be oblivious or in the dark. Be awake, assertive, and pay attention! First Peter 5:8 tells us, "Be alert and of sober mind" so that we are conscious of Satan's tactics.

2. The flesh is weak.

Be cognizant of what sin area burdens you. You're not naïve; you know what you struggle with. Some struggle with lust. Others, like our many SEC cases, struggle with materialism and greed. Others struggle with vanity and narcissism. Still others struggle with anger issues. Whatever your sin struggle is, be aware of it and own it.

Armed with a strong self-awareness of what sins cause you to stumble, be diligent to keep them at arm's length. Apply the arm's length principle—don't allow your tests to enter your embrace, causing them to escalate to a temptation. Keep your tests tests.

This week, you are bound to face a test. It could be a test to treat someone who frustrates you with disrespect, or to fudge the numbers a bit at work, or to view something online that you shouldn't, or to fall back into an old habit or addiction.

Whatever it is, let's all watch and pray so that we're aware of our tests. Let's realize that our flesh is weak and own up to our struggle. Then let's apply the arm's length principle in order to keep our tests tests. Let's handle life's tests in a way that glorifies and honors our Heavenly Father!

THIS WEEK, STRIVE...

☐ To identify one test in your life. It could be greed, lust, power, pride, needing acceptance, or many others. These are only the beginning of the possibilities. Own the test. Admit your struggle to yourself. Then, think back the "Familiar Territory" Strive challenges in Week 7. Did you establish an accountability relationship? If not, this could be the week! Consider who could regularly hold you accountable to overcome your test.

☐ To be on the lookout for your test all around you each day this week. Watch and pray for help understanding where the test is lurking. Ask God to reveal where downfalls may lie. Take note of your urges to make the test a temptation. Be aware of your surroundings. How could an accountability partner support you?

☐ To apply the arm's length principle. If there's a certain person or place that pushes the test toward temptation, do you need to consider discontinuing the relationship or changing your environment? If certain technology or possessions make a test cross the temptation line, how can you set better boundaries? Be diligent in prayer for God's strength as you make changes. It won't be easy, but it will be worth it!

EYE CONTACT
WEEK 40

Now a man who was lame from birth was being carried to the temple gate called Beautiful, where he was put every day to beg from those going into the temple courts. When he saw Peter and John about to enter, he asked them for money. Peter looked straight at him, as did John. Then Peter said, "Look at us!" So the man gave them his attention, expecting to get something from them. Then Peter said, "Silver or gold I do not have, but what I do have I give you. In the name of Jesus Christ of Nazareth, walk."

ACTS 3:2–6

I was walking down a busy street in Chicago. People flooded both sides of the street, ducking in and out of shops and restaurants. I had just crossed the street and was stepping up onto the curb of the sidewalk. On the corner of the sidewalk there were three or four newspaper vending machines offering the daily news for a couple of quarters.

A man sat on the ground, slumped, leaning against the newspaper vending machines. He looked exhausted, hot, and beaten down by life's circumstances. He had no shoes, but was wearing makeshift cardboard sandals. His jeans were dirty, ripped, and too short. He donned a stretched out sweater on his upper body and a black stocking cap on his head. By his side was a plastic cup partially filled with change and a couple of dollar bills. A rumpled cardboard sign leaned on the base of the newspaper vending machines.

"Homeless. Please help."

I put my head down, quickened my pace, and walked on by, completely avoiding eye contact.

You've been there before, haven't you? The awkward moment when some homeless stranger is in your path. That uncomfortable encounter between your personal agenda and someone else's immediate needs. What do you do?

During a personal study of the book of Acts, the beginning of the third chapter really caught my eye. I must have read these opening verses four or five times before. But my Chicago experience brought their words flooding back to memory. I began comparing and contrasting Peter's and John's interaction with the beggar at the temple gate to my avoidance of the man by the newspaper vending machines. One thing stood out: "Peter looked straight at him, as did John. Then Peter said, 'Look at us!' So the man gave them his attention."

It all starts with eye contact. A group of psychologists ran a study on eye contact in a speed-dating setting. Men and women who were total strangers showed up to a social mixer evening at a hotel, hoping to find a companion. But the men had received some coaching from the researchers about how much eye contact to make throughout the evening—some lots, others little. After the event, the researchers polled all the female participants.

The results? Those who received the most eye contact from the men felt the deepest level of connection, affection, and a sense of being appreciated.

Eye contact is a beginning indicator of love.

Jesus himself put love above all other commands and teachings during his time on earth:

> "Teacher, which is the greatest commandment in the Law?" Jesus replied: "'Love the Lord your God with all your heart and with all your soul and with all your mind.' This is the first and greatest commandment. And the second is like it: 'Love your neighbor as yourself.'" (Matthew 22:36–39)

So I find it interesting that Peter and John, who spent three years of their life following Jesus' every move, both "looked straight at" the beggar at the gate. And in fact, they go so far as to demand his eye contact in return: "Peter said, 'Look at us!' So the man gave them his attention."

Peter and John don't give the beggar money. They don't give him food. They give him their eyes. And in so doing, I believe they gave him the love of Jesus by the power of the Holy Spirit in their hearts.

The next time you're in my situation on the street, don't ignore the man or woman in need. Give them the dignity, love, and the respect of Christ through your eye contact. Being willing to look them in the eye says, "You're worth something. You have value. I love you." Perhaps, the Spirit will even lead you to pray with them or to share your faith. But start with eye contact, an indicator of love for the sake of Jesus Christ.

This week, Strive...

☐ To make eye contact with as many people as possible in your coming and going this week. At work, at the store, at church, at your appointments, don't look down at your papers, pull out your phone, or look past them. Simply acknowledge others' presence wherever you go.

☐ To evaluate the results of your eye contact experiment. Was it easy? Was it awkward? What did you notice about yourself? (I was amazed how often I look past others in my busyness!) How did others react? Did they reciprocate eye contact or smile? Was eye contact well received?

☐ To pray for God's guidance around how you can better love others. It could be as simple and practical as making eye contact, smiling, or putting down what you're doing to fully listen. It could involve praying for a specific person or people. Maybe you're being called to meet the needs of someone else spiritually, emotionally, or in a physical sense with food or clothing. Let's do all we can to love our neighbors!

PUT YOUR MONEY
WHERE YOUR MOUTH IS
WEEK 41

*"Will a mere mortal rob God? Yet you rob me. But you ask, 'How are
we robbing you?' In tithes and offerings. You are under a curse—your
whole nation—because you are robbing me. Bring the whole tithe into
the storehouse, that there may be food in my house. Test me in this,"
says the LORD Almighty, "and see if I will not throw open the floodgates
of heaven and pour out so much blessing that there will not be room
enough to store it."*

MALACHI 3:8–10

It's a raucous time of preseason high school football: equipment issue
day. It's not one of the reasons I enjoy coaching. Young men come flock-
ing in to be sized for helmets, shoulder pads, and other football-related
goodies. Picture about one hundred rabid, hyper, five-year-olds on
Christmas morning. That's what it's like.

I hear a lot of gratitude on equipment day, but I also hear a lot of
complaining.

"I didn't get a new helmet."

"I didn't get the facemask I wanted."

"These pads don't fit."

"I wanted a different number."

"This has a rip in it."

"I don't like this one."

My knee-jerk inner reaction to all this complaining is to give out
choke holds rather than practice jerseys to our players. But I refrain.
Instead, I played a new angle with each complainer this year:

"If you don't like what you've been given," I said, "may I remind you
that we take donations around here to help us buy better equipment for

the program. If you're passionate about that cause, I'd strongly encourage you to put your money where your mouth is."

The complaints stopped pretty quickly. Not too many fifteen-year-olds have the budget to afford helmets that cost $250 a piece!

But now I turn to you who are reading this. (I can hear you "gulping" as you wonder what I'm going to say next.)

Are you passionate about Jesus? If you are, I'd strongly encourage you to put your money where your mouth is. Are you?

This is the part of faith where the rubber meets the road, where your faith is no longer your father's or mother's or family's or friends' faith. This is where a nebulous big idea becomes your real personal faith in Jesus.

If you're proclaiming Jesus as Lord of all, is he the Lord of your checkbook and wallet too?

My wife and I learned to trust our finances to God during a hard point in our life: a time of unemployment. I had been cut by the Indianapolis Colts and was in search of a new team. During this time of transition and uncertainty, my wife and I decided the best "home base" for us was a one-bedroom apartment in her hometown in Michigan until I got another call. We were excited to be settled after the whirlwind of living in team hotels and being unsure of what was next.

But we now had new bills and no jobs or steady income. It was a humbling reality and stark difference from being on an NFL roster.

It was during this season of life that our pastor preached an extremely convicting sermon on a spiritual discipline my wife and I had not yet begun in our young marriage: tithing, giving generously of our earnings to God's Kingdom work through the church.

Our pastor cited scripture from Malachi chapter 3, the only place in the Bible where God challenges us to test him and his goodness:

"'Bring the whole tithe into the storehouse, that there may be food in my house. Test me in this,' says the Lord Almighty, 'and see if I will not throw open the floodgates of heaven and pour out so much blessing that there will not be room enough to store it'" (v. 10).

Unsure of how we were going to pull off this new practice, but knowing we needed to trust in God's word, I did a little math, and we started giving systematically to our church.

Then about ten days later on a Thursday evening, we were eating dinner when my wife's phone rang. She was getting ready to start substitute teaching, as the school year was in full swing that fall. It was the principal from a local elementary school offering her a full-time teaching job.

Then a couple of weeks later, I was offered a work opportunity with the flexibility to keep training for my next NFL opportunity, and I got to coach football at a local high school in the evenings. Eventually, I got a couple more cracks at fulfilling my NFL dream.

As time has moved on, beyond the NFL and those uncertain times, God has provided us with other job opportunities and with enough financial provision to own a home and to meet and far exceed our needs. And there is always enough to keep giving generously to his Kingdom work in the world.

Please do not misinterpret what I am saying here. The jobs, finances, and the possessions are not the pursuit. They are just things. The pursuit is God and making him Lord of all, even your finances. In the process of fully pursuing him with everything you have, he takes care of your needs.

Today, whether you practice tithing or haven't taken that step of faith yet, I urge you to take God at his word. Accept his challenge. Commit everything you have to him, even your finances. See what great and mighty works he can do—both in your life and in the lives of others!

THIS WEEK, STRIVE...

- ☐ To thank God each day for his provision in your life. He is the source of and the reason for everything you have. Does he know you are grateful?
- ☐ To read Malachi 3:8–10 each day this week. Reflect and meditate on these verses and the difficult question they pose: How are you "robbing" God? Make note of what he reveals to you. Where do you need to be more generous and "test" him and his goodness?

☐ To evaluate your giving practices. Are you tithing and already giving back to the Lord what is his? Start prayerfully considering how you might increase your level of giving, even by 1 or 2 percent. Is giving yet to be a practice of yours? Start planning, through prayer, how you can work toward regularly giving to further the work of the Gospel.

BELIEVERS? OR KNOWERS?
WEEK 42

Not everyone who says to me, "Lord, Lord," will enter the kingdom of heaven, but only the one who does the will of my Father who is in heaven. Many will say to me on that day, "Lord, Lord, did we not prophesy in your name and in your name drive out demons and in your name perform many miracles?" Then I will tell them plainly, "I never knew you. Away from me, you evildoers!"

MATTHEW 7:21–23

The more I think about it, the more I don't really know why Christ followers call themselves "believers." Aren't we called to be so much more than that?

Yes, we must believe in Jesus by faith, that he is the son of God, died on the cross for our sin, and rose from the dead. Believing is important. But isn't there more to following Jesus than just belief?

After all, James 2:19 reminds us, "You believe that there is one God. Good! Even the demons believe that—and shudder."

Even Satan's demons are believers!

I'd like to suggest that rather than believers, we must be *knowers* of the one true God. Jesus offers some sobering words in this week's passage from Matthew 7. Notice three key statements:

1. "NOT EVERYONE WHO SAYS TO ME, 'LORD, LORD,' WILL ENTER THE KINGDOM OF HEAVEN."

Jesus says that many people who do not enter the kingdom of heaven are in fact believers! They call Jesus "Lord, Lord!" They understand who he is. They realize he is the son of God. They believe in him.

Furthermore, these individuals display emotional attachment to and involvement with Jesus. In ancient Greek, repetitive language ("Lord, Lord!") signified a demonstrative and passionate appeal. These people feel a connection to Christ, yet they are on the outside looking in.

2. "DID WE NOT PROPHESY IN YOUR NAME AND IN YOUR NAME DRIVE OUT DEMONS AND IN YOUR NAME PERFORM MANY MIRACLES?"

Not only are these people believers, but they are doing things for Jesus! They are taking action in his name—prophesying, driving out demons, performing miracles. They are acting on what they believe. By outward appearances, it seems they are doing everything right.

3. "THEN I WILL TELL THEM PLAINLY, 'I NEVER KNEW YOU. AWAY FROM ME, YOU EVILDOERS!'"

But then Jesus drops the bomb: "I never knew you."

You believe in me. You understand who I am. I make you emotional. You realize I am God's son. You are even taking action—action that aligns with your beliefs and is helping other people and making a difference.

But you never truly, personally knew me.

Don't miss this today. Belief, understanding, realization, and action are *not* enough, unless we truly know Jesus.

Do you know him? And if you do, does it show?

In following Jesus, we have a relationship, not a religion. We have a friend, not a figurehead. We have a brother, not a boss. And his desire is for you to know him as deeply as he knows you. Because he made you, loves you, and redeemed your life.

Relationships take time, effort, and investment. They require asking tough questions, listening, and learning; sacrifice and submission; love and care. Relationships require work!

Are you putting in the work? Is there evidence in your actions that you are being conformed into the image of Christ?

This week, invest in the effort to know Jesus better than you did last week. Today, spend a few extra minutes with him in prayer, asking him to reveal himself more and more to you. Do the same tomorrow, and the next day, and the day after that.

Let's be more than just believers. Let's be knowers!

THIS WEEK, STRIVE...

☐ To think about how you would define *belief* and how you would define *knowing*. Would you rather have someone say they believe you can accomplish something, or that they know you'll get the job done? Is one stronger than the other? What do these words convey to you?

☐ To assess the motives behind the acts of service or generosity you perform. Why do you serve? Why do you give? Is it an overflow of knowing your Heavenly Father? Are your motivations properly placed?

☐ To identify what you find most convicting about Matthew 7:21–23. Is there a change you need to make? Do you need to spend some time with God this week? Take time to pray that God would use your conviction for his glory.

THE CALL
WEEK 43

The angel of the LORD came and sat down under the oak in Ophrah that belonged to Joash the Abiezrite, where his son Gideon was thresh-ing wheat in a winepress to keep it from the Midianites. When the angel of the LORD appeared to Gideon, he said, "The LORD is with you, mighty warrior."... "Pardon me, my lord," Gideon replied, "but how can I save Israel? My clan is the weakest in Manasseh, and I am the least in my family." The LORD answered, "I will be with you, and you will strike down all the Midianites, leaving none alive."

JUDGES 6:11–16

He's the most unlikely of heroes but a hero just the same. We'll call him Sam.

Sam was a member of the first two teams I coached as a head football coach. In many ways, Sam was a typical teenager, navigating the usual daily issues of social life, school, and sports. On the other hand, Sam was completely different.

Sam has cerebral palsy. Due to his CP, Sam has limited use of the entire right side of his body. I think it's safe to say a lot of medical profes-sionals would've shuddered at Sam running around on a full-contact football field. But I've seen Sam run sprints, lift weights, tackle oppo-nents, catch footballs, and even bear-crawl on all fours—with essentially one arm.

His heart is bigger than his disability. On paper Sam wasn't cut from the cloth of a football player. But because of his heart, the final game of the year I decided to make *the call*.

"Sam! Head in at running back."

I can only imagine what they were saying about me in the stands at that point!

"Coach, I can't!"

Overcome with emotion, nerves, excitement, and fear, it took two plays, three coaches, and a handful of players to convince a tearful Sam that it was his time to go in. He was ready for this moment.

It was his time to answer the call. On the night of the final football game of his life, Sam carried the ball three times, to the tune of a wildly chanting student section.

Gideon was probably the most unlikely hero of his time. He was from one of the weakest tribes of Israel—Manasseh—which was really a spin-off of the tribe of Joseph, split into two smaller groups by Joseph's sons Ephraim and Manasseh. Not only was Gideon from a weak tribe, but his clan was "the weakest in Manasseh," a weak clan in which he was "the least in [his] family."

But then came the call. Off the sidelines and into the game. "The LORD is with you, mighty warrior."

Mighty warrior? Gideon was not a mighty warrior. This guy was the least of the least of the least, just threshing the wheat at the family farm. He was a nobody, and he says so himself. "Pardon me, my lord, …but how can I save Israel?" Translation: "God, I'm not cut out for this job."

It doesn't matter, Gideon. You've been called.

So have we. We are what God calls us to be. Even if we're not what he's calling us to be, we are. Because he called us. God has a track record with this type of thing:

- Childless Abraham called to be a father
- Shy, scared, stammering public speaker Moses called to lead a nation
- Slave Joseph called to political power in order to save thousands from starvation
- Young shepherd David called to kill a giant and become a king
- Christian execution artist Saul called to be Christian leader Paul

God doesn't call the qualified. He qualifies the called.

Today, like Sam and Gideon, I'm certain there is something in your

life that God, through his word, is calling you to take on—and you feel
ill-prepared to do it. Maybe it's becoming more consistent with your daily
time in the word and prayer, or having a difficult conversation you know
is necessary, or proceeding with a daunting assignment at work, or doing
a better job as a parent.

Whatever it is, even if you feel unprepared, the call is what matters.
If you've been called, you're equipped. Period. Take on the challenge
with confidence! God is with you. You have all you need.

THIS WEEK, STRIVE...

- ☐ To read Gideon's story in Judges chapters 6, 7, and 8. What are
  the key themes of Gideon's life? What do you notice about the
  way God works through Gideon?
- ☐ To reflect on Gideon's story and God's track record of qualifying
  those he calls to do his work. What is one intimidating, audacious, daunting task that God is calling you to take on in your
  life? Do you trust him to equip you for the task?
- ☐ To write down the doubts you have around the big task God is
  calling you to take on. List each one, then pray through the list
  line by line, asking God for power to overcome your doubts by
  faith. In him you have everything you need.

SPECIAL FRIEND
WEEK 44

Accept one another, then, just as Christ accepted you, in order to bring praise to God.

ROMANS 15:7

One of the highlights of my year came from an unlikely source: Special Persons Day at a local elementary school.

A dear friend of our family's fifth-grade son invited me to be his "special person" for the afternoon, to which I gladly obliged. On arrival at the busy, bustling school building, my young host introduced me to his classmates.

"This is Tim," he said, "and he's a friend of our family."

There was a lingering pause in the air, the kind that sounds like, "And...? Yes,...go on..."

My young host didn't sense this pause at all. He was content with the introduction and was ready to take me on a tour of the school building. But as we turned to exit the classroom, his teacher pressed him a bit.

"And why is he special?" his teacher asked. She was attempting to subtly hint at my football background and athletic endeavors.

"This ought to be really, really good," I thought to myself with a smile.

It was more than good. His response was great. It exemplified true, loving friendship.

"Because he's a friend of our family," he responded.

"I know that," the teacher said. "But why is he special?" She made what appeared to be a football throwing motion with her right arm.

Clearly, my friend just wasn't quite catching her drift.

"Because he's our friend," my young host emphatically answered.

What a wise and true answer. (Isn't it amazing how kids get this stuff and we adults miss it?)

I started thinking about why I have value in the eyes other people. Have you ever taken time to consider this? Isn't it true that, in many cases, people think you're special because:

- You have money?
- You have connections that can help them?
- You have notoriety or success?
- You have something they want?

But here I was in a fifth grade classroom with my young friend, and I learn that I am special to him just because I am his friend. Not because of any merits or accolades, or anything I've done for him, said to him, given him, or anything I've earned.

I am special to him, just because I am who I am. Is that cool or what?

Isn't that what we are all looking for in this life? A friend who doesn't want our stuff but wants us just as we are, who thinks we're worth his or her time, who thinks we're special for who we are. Does this type of friend even exist?

Yes, that type of friend does exist.

Kathy Keller, wife of Timothy Keller, pastor of Redeemer Presbyterian Church in New York City, has been a life-long C. S. Lewis fan. As a young girl, she read all Lewis's children's books and decided to write him several letters. By age fifteen, she had written Lewis four letters about his books.

He personally responded to all four letters. Three were handwritten, the fourth was typed because Lewis's health was failing and he had someone compose it for him. He responded to Kathy Keller's final letter just a month before his death.

Keller makes an astounding point from this exchange of letters. If a gifted and influential writer would care enough about a teenage girl he never met to take the time to communicate with her, how much more does Jesus Christ care about people he created and knows deeply?

How special are we in the eyes of Christ? We are special to him, just because we are who we are. That friend does exist. Jesus is that special friend.

Today, let's live out Romans 15:7. Take time to marvel at the ultimate price Christ paid for you in order to accept you as special to him. Then go accept others as special for who they are—all for the glory of God.

THIS WEEK, STRIVE...

- ☐ To think about someone you admire deeply. Why do you think highly of that person? What core attributes draws you to him or her?
- ☐ To consider why you desire a relationship with this admired person. Is it because of whom he or she knows, possesses, or has accomplished? Or is it just because of who this person is?
- ☐ To now consider your relationship with Jesus Christ. He admires you, loves you, even died for you. Do you think fondly of him? Do you want to know him? Or do you just want his provision with no relationship? Write down one practical way you will seek to know him better this week.

WHO DO YOU THINK YOU ARE?
WEEK 45

Then Peter began to speak: "I now realize how true it is that God does not show favoritism but accepts from every nation the one who fears him and does what is right."

ACTS 10:34–35

The president of a prominent, faith-based institution of higher learning was entering the grocery store. It was the Christmas season. Garland, ribbon, and white lights lined the storefront as the university president strolled in. Carols were playing from the speakers of the store's front entrance. There was a familiar ringing in the air, the Salvation Army donation bell.

A short woman in her late sixties wearing a Santa hat stood bundled up outside the entrance to the store. She smiled and greeted each guest, thanking them for their donations. Occasionally, the president noticed she would engage in some dialogue with a store guest before the customer proceeded into the store.

The president stopped about twenty feet away from the red kettle and reached into his pocket. He opened his wallet, thumbed through his cash, and pulled out a couple of bills. He folded them in half, then in half again to fit the donation kettle's small opening. As he approached the entrance he smiled and greeted the volunteer ringing the bell and then paused and leaned forward to insert his donation.

"Sir, are you saved?"

The question from the volunteer jolted the president a bit. Apparently, this was the dialogue he saw her engaging in with other customers. He stood upright to meet the eye contact of the bell ringer. Caught off guard by her boldness, he did everything he could to remain cordial and calm.

"Why, yes," he responded with a warm smile. "I suppose I am."

Not totally satisfied with his "suppose" answer, the woman pressed further. "Well, sir, I mean, have you fully given your life to the Lord?"

In response to her persistence, the president felt the time was right to reveal his identity to the Salvation Army volunteer. *She must not know who I am,* he thought to himself. *After all, I am a pretty prominent figure in our community.* Smiling again, the president cleared his throat to respond. "I am the president of the local university," he said as politely as possible. "And in addition, I am the head of the seminary program there."

"Oh," the woman said quietly. She looked back and forth at the ground for a moment as she pondered his statement. Her gaze returned to his eyes.

"That's okay," she replied. "It doesn't matter who you are or where you've been. You can still be saved."

What a great response!

What was the president really saying when he revealed his identity? *Don't you know who I am? Of course I know Jesus; I'm the head of a seminary!*

And…your point is…?

How much do you think it appalls God when we say or think things like:

Don't you know who I am? Of course I know Jesus, because

———————————————.

- I serve at the homeless shelter every Tuesday night.
- My family has been going to church there for three generations.
- I've been a Sunday School teacher for twenty years.
- I pray before I eat, even in public.
- The pastor is a really good friend of mine.
- I've never broken the law and I live a decent life.

Even in the disciple Peter's time, people played the "Don't you know who I am?" card all the time. It was just a little different.

Don't you know who I am? Of course I know God, because I'm Jewish.

Jews were chosen. Jews "knew" God. Not Gentiles. They were unclean outcasts, scorned by mainstream society. But then, God speaks to Peter through a vision and blows the doors off the "Don't you know who I am?" line of logic:

"Do not call anything impure that God has made clean" (Acts 10:15).

The Lord tells Peter, a Jew, to share the Gospel with Cornelius, a Gentile, who, with his entire household, become the first Gentiles to receive the Holy Spirit and experience personal conversion to follow Jesus Christ. Humbled and astonished, Peter would say:

"I now realize how true it is that God does not show favoritism but accepts from every nation the one who fears him and does what is right" (vv. 34–35).

Last time I checked, showing a "spiritual ID" doesn't save you. Showing your spiritual driver's license or résumé might get you into church these days, but certainly not into Heaven.

Faith in Jesus Christ saves you. Period. No matter who you are, where you've been, or what you've done. His death and resurrection alone have the power to redeem you and me.

Do you know him?

This week, as we live our lives and as we minister to others, let's humble ourselves. Our spiritual résumé is but "filthy rags" (Isaiah 64:6) before our Holy God. Let's not play the spiritual "Don't you know who I am?" card. Rather, let's all be able to live out the criteria God gave to Peter:

"Of course I know Jesus, because I fear God and do what is right."

THIS WEEK, STRIVE...

☐ To repent for the times where you've grown prideful about your "good works"—your volunteer work, your giving, or your church attendance record. Ask God for his patience and forgiveness.

☐ To read Isaiah 64:5–8 three times this week. How do these verses humble you? How do they encourage you?

☐ To honestly answer the Salvation Army volunteer's question: "Are you saved?" Have you placed your faith in Jesus and welcomed him into your life? If not, what doubts, fears, or hesitations are holding you back? Is it time to make a decision to follow Christ?

PARTING WORDS
WEEK 46

Do not let any unwholesome talk come out of your mouths, but only what is helpful for building others up according to their needs, that it may benefit those who listen.

EPHESIANS 4:29

Why is it that our best words are typically parting words? Consider three examples that demonstrate what I mean.

As a high school football coach, I am invited to more graduation parties each spring than I've had birthday parties in a lifetime. By the first week of June, the invitation stack on the kitchen counter is easily an inch thick. Because there's not a chance I can make every party, I've made it my practice to write a handwritten, personal letter to each graduate who invites me to an open house. In each letter I attempt to remind the student of something important to carry with him or her beyond high school. I do all I can to inspire confidence as the student leaves this chapter of life. I sincerely remind the student what wonderful gifts he or she possesses and make suggestions on using those gifts to make a difference in the world before them.

Since my football career ended, I have changed jobs several times. With any job change comes what I call the "farewell tour"—that somewhat awkward time after you announce your departure where you repeat yourself about 1,500 times regarding your new job—where it is, what your title is, your future plans and goals, and so on. After a day passed and my vocal cords came back, I was amazed to find how cluttered my inbox was with hundreds of e-mails from people (I hate to admit this) whom I didn't even know, all filled with "good lucks" and "best wishes" and "thanks for all you do's," and even many filled with very deep, touching, personal sentiments.

A few years ago, my father's parents both went home to Heaven within about six months of each other. Our family was deeply touched by the outpouring of support at both rounds of calling hours and at both funerals. Out-of-town family, friends, and community members came in droves to pay their respects and tributes to two wonderful people. I remember being amazed by the emotions and unbelievably kind words people spoke about my grandparents. I wasn't amazed so much that these things were being said—my grandparents were two wonderful human beings. Rather, I was amazed by who was saying them. I'd never heard some of these people say things so heartfelt, kind, and meaningful.

Why is it that we save our best, most genuine, encouraging and uplifting words for when people are leaving? Why only for parting words?

Why do I wait to share how I feel about my players until after they graduate? Why wouldn't I tell them how great they are and what difference makers they can be while they're still playing for me?

Why did my colleagues come out of the woodwork after I left my job? Why didn't they send me well wishes, encouragement, and kind words while I was still working with them?

Why did so many family, friends, and community members share their most loving words about my grandparents at their calling hours and funerals? Why didn't they share their deepest thoughts and feelings while they were still living?

Why is it that our best words are typically parting words?

What if we spoke a few of our best words every day, if we transformed the way we communicate with one another and shared the way we truly feel with one person each day? What if we followed the Apostle Paul's counsel in Ephesians 4:29, if we never "let any unwholesome talk come out of [our] mouths," and only said things "helpful for building others up according to their needs" that would "benefit those who listen"?

How much better would our homes, workplaces, hospitals, classrooms, churches, communities, and our lives be if we stopped saving our best words for parting words?

Today, let's stop asking "What if?" Let's create a new reality and spend a few of our best words on someone else today and every day. Don't wait until your most heartfelt words end up being parting words. Let's honor Jesus with words "helpful for building others up according to their needs." May we be men and women whose every word will "benefit those who listen."

THIS WEEK, STRIVE...

☐ To identify one person with whom you need to share a good word of encouragement, an expression of gratitude, or a note about how much they mean to you. Then go do it! Don't wait for these kind words to be parting words.

☐ To reflect on the good word you shared with someone this week. What was hard or uncomfortable about this experience? What was fulfilling and edifying about it? What will it take for you to make this a regular habit?

☐ To build into your calendar, phone, planner, or schedule a weekly reminder to share a good word with someone every week. Make it a recurring event in your agenda so it becomes an engrained habit.

PRIDE IN DISGUISE
WEEK 47

*For the Spirit God gave us does not make us timid, but gives us power,
love and self-discipline.*

2 TIMOTHY 1:7

In a recent meeting at work, we discussed one issue at great length. It
wasn't a matter of life or death, or anything that compromised anyone's
values. But as I listened to the opinions of the group, I had an inner conviction about the right way to handle it.

But I didn't say anything. I found myself caught in a mental battle
over whether my opinion would be valid and if people would receive
my ideas well, and what the group might think of me or say in response
to my interjection.

It was a classic case of paralysis by analysis. I was timid and decided
not to speak up as I should have.

Second Timothy 1:7 tells us that if we are walking with Jesus, God's
Holy Spirit within us "does not make us timid." If you are following Jesus,
there is not timidity within you. The Holy Spirit is not timid. It does not
fear the unfamiliar or unknown. It is not afraid to stand for what is right
and true.

So what is the source of the timidity we feel at times? The Lord didn't
give it to us. The Bible tells us that we aren't hardwired by our Creator to
be timid. But there has to be a root cause. Where does it come from? Pride.

Timidity is pride in disguise. When we are timid, we are really
being prideful because our concern is not about the good of others.
Our concern is about what others think of us or what might happen
to us. It is self-perception over service, timidity over truth, and easy
over right.

The harsh reality is that pride is the root that produces the vicious, spreading weed of sin in our thoughts, words, and deeds. I'd even go so far to say that pride is at the very core and origin of *all* sin in our lives.

What are we to do? Look upon the cross.

When I was a freshman on the football team at Western Michigan University, we had a six a.m. workout one morning for all of us who were "red-shirting," that is, delaying participation in game competition for a season but lengthening eligibility by a year, to help young athletes develop. There were about twenty-five of us in the group, but only twenty-four were present. Someone was missing, but our coach proceeded with the workout, not saying a word.

After practice that evening, all the freshmen were asked to stay after. This time, twenty-five were present. The punishment was doled out for one of us being absent—a dreaded 250 up-downs. (If you don't know what on earth an up-down is, be grateful!) But there was one caveat to the penalty. Our teammate who slept through the workout had to stand in the middle of the twenty-four of us and watch as *we* did the punishment he deserved. Nothing is more humbling than helplessly watching others being punished in your place.

But that's exactly what Jesus did. He "bore our sins in his body" (1 Peter 2:24). He was beaten, spit on, flogged, nailed, pierced, and painfully pinned to the rugged cross for our sake. Our sin put him there.

If we take time daily to dwell on his sacrifice and be grateful for it, we will put pride out of our lives. In so doing we will slowly pluck the root that produces timidity, greed, rebellion, mistreatment, selfishness, and stubbornness in us.

Today, look on the cross of Christ, the ultimate source of humility.

THIS WEEK, STRIVE...

- ☐ To identify one way pride regularly creeps into your life. Is it a more obvious way, like ego, power, or greed? Or is it subtle, like judgmentalism or timidity? What are the effects on you?
- ☐ To recall a situation in which you "got off the hook" and didn't get what you deserved. Did someone forgive you? Did you receive a gift? Was a punishment turned into a teachable

moment? What happened? How did it make you feel? What did you learn?

☐ To memorize 1 Peter 2:24. How will you show gratitude for what Jesus has done for us?

WASTING TIME
WEEK 48

Be very careful, then, how you live—not as unwise but as wise, making the most of every opportunity, because the days are evil.

EPHESIANS 5:15–16

The 40-hour work week is dead. We know this well, do we not? According the Bureau of Labor Statistics, Americans ages twenty-five to fifty-four work an average of 8.8 hours a day, or 44 hours a week, based on a five-day work week (which is dying too!).[1] Factor in our constant connection to laptops, tablets, and smartphones, and that weekly average easily shoots up to 55 hours of work or more.

The 40-hour television week, however, is alive and well. According to Nielsen's Media and Entertainment Report, Americans spend an average of almost 5.5 hours a day, more than 41 hours a week, viewing video content on a screen. This 41-hour number includes TV, DVR playback, video games, and watching DVDs. It does not account for time on the computer, e-mail, and social media.[2]

So, in essence, the average American has two full-time jobs. We are full-time workers and full-time screen watchers.

In his letter to the church at Ephesus, the Apostle Paul writes that we must be cautious with our lives, live wisely, and maximize the time we're given. Why? "Because the days are evil."

Most commentaries I've read interpret this phrase to mean, "Because times are desperate," the human race is going down a bad path and society frantically needs the good news of the Gospel of Jesus Christ. Thus, we should make the most of our time here on earth to make disciples and share our faith in Jesus with others. It's what the world fervently needs.

I completely and wholeheartedly agree with the commentators. But

I also think "the days are evil" has another implied meaning: that time is not on our side. There is no time to waste.

I believe that when we make the choice to prioritize and maximize the time we are given, no matter how limited it is, we can achieve great results if we don't waste that time.

Given the statistics we've reviewed, consider this:

There are 168 hours in a week. Carve out 50 hours for work, 56 hours for sleep, and the staggering 41 hours for screen watching that Nielsen reports, and you are left with 21 extra hours for the week. That's three hours a day. And you haven't factored in any meals, any social interaction, or any time with God in prayer or reading his word!

I'm not saying don't watch TV or take time to relax. You work hard. For Pete's sake, vege out on the couch a little bit now and then! You deserve it. But I am begging you to consider a powerful question: What are you doing with your limited time on earth? Is it blowing by you as you sit at your desk, then sit on your couch, then lie in your bed? Or are you "making the most of every opportunity"?

Just think about what could be done with the 41 hours a week wasted in front of a screen. Instead, Americans could: have family dinner, spend more time in God's word, start a new company, have an impactful conversation with a neighbor or friend, go for a walk or run, find an accountability partner, start a new nonprofit, volunteer, serve on a community board, join a Bible study, workout more, write a book, help more at church, build better relationships, spend more time with our children, start a blog, improve our marriages, get our finances back on track, read a new book, take a class . . .

We would be healthier, smarter, more joyful, more fit, and more on fire for Christ. We would be better. And a BETTER US + JESUS CHRIST = A MORE POWERFUL IMPACT.

The world would truly be a better place.

This week, commit the words of Psalm 89:47 to memory: "Remember how fleeting is my life." Consider how you're spending your time. Are you wasting it? Let's not waste another hour. Let's take on Paul's challenge—"Be very careful, then, how you live—not as unwise but as wise, making the most of every opportunity."

THIS WEEK, STRIVE...

- ☐ To list the top three ways you spend your discretionary time. Think about how much of it is spent in front of a screen of some sort—TV, phone, tablet, computer, and more. As you evaluate your time budget, are you wasting any time? What pockets of time could be better utilized?
- ☐ To pray over your discretionary-time activities list each day this week. Ask God to use the list as he sees fit. Surrender it to him. Dare to give him control of your time and see what he does with it. What is stirring in your heart and mind as you pray?
- ☐ To identify one thing you feel God laying on your heart and mind as you pray about your time. What's the one thing you know you should do that you keep postponing or putting off with the excuse "I don't have enough time." Is God calling you to that? Where can you serve him best with the time you have?

How Do You View Him?
Week 49

Philip found Nathanael and told him, "We have found the one Moses wrote about in the Law, and about whom the prophets also wrote— Jesus of Nazareth, the son of Joseph." "Nazareth! Can anything good come from there?" Nathanael asked. "Come and see," said Philip.

JOHN 1:45–46

"Are you crazy?"

I was standing with a good friend of mine, looking at a large sand dune that was uniquely situated on the corner of a residential neighborhood in northwest Florida. In addition to its strange location, I was drawn to the large mound of beach for another reason.

It was perfect for a workout. All I could think about were the endless possibilities for cardio and conditioning, like sprints, bounding, plyometrics, and over-speed training. There was tremendous potential right before us! My mind was brimming with the prospects for breaking a good sweat.

I verbalized my vision to my friend standing beside me. As he processed my idea while eyeballing the dune's white granules, something became very evident. My friend clearly didn't share my viewpoint.

"The only thing that hill is good for is sliding down it," he retorted. He went on to list all the creative and outside-the-box ways you could descend down the mountain of shoreline—inner tube, beach bike, cafeteria tray greased with cooking spray, and plywood board. Clearly he had thought about this before. We laughed as we left the dune behind, both resisting our temptations to run up or slide down the sandy hill.

As I reflected on our exchange about the sand dune, I was struck by something: We were both looking at the exact same thing, but we had completely different views of it.

We encounter this every day. In this life we tend to view situations, circumstances, places, and people very differently. How we view things greatly affects our attitude, disposition, and actions as we live and move through the world.

But there is one particular person on whom we all must formulate a viewpoint that has ramifications for this life and all eternity: the person of Jesus Christ. How do you view him?

In the early stages of John's gospel we find two men formulating this important view of Jesus—Philip and Nathanael. Philip exclaims: "We have found the one Moses wrote about in the Law, and about whom the prophets also wrote—Jesus of Nazareth, the son of Joseph."

In other words, "This Jesus—he's the real deal! He's the son of God, the Messiah!"

But Nathanael is not so chipper: "Nazareth! Can anything good come from there?"

It's a fair question. For the believer reading this, I'm confident you've come across a skeptic who responds to your faith in a Nathanael-like manner. For the one who is spiritually uncertain and reading this, you understand Nathanael's line of reason and cynicism. Can this Jesus be real?

But the value to us all, no matter our spiritual convictions, comes in the wisdom of Philip's response: "Come and see."

There is no forcing of views. There is no condemnation, arguing, debating, or pushing. Simply, "come and see." Do the research. Check it out for yourself. Examine the evidence at hand. Then make your own decision.

Today, I urge you to answer two questions for yourself:

1. HOW DO YOU VIEW JESUS?

Is he the king of your life, or are you sitting on his throne instead?

2. HOW DO YOU REACT TO OTHERS WHO DO NOT SHARE YOUR VIEW?

Are you negative, condescending, condemning, or judgmental, or do you invite them to "come and see"?

No matter where you stand, today, learn from Philip's example, and also take Jeremiah 29:13 to heart: "You will seek me and find me when you seek me with all your heart." God promises that when we truly "come and see," we will indeed find him.

THIS WEEK, STRIVE...

- [ ] To select one person, place, or thing that you've been viewing with a negative attitude. Ask for God's help in making the selection. Then consider changing your vantage point. Is there another side to the story? Are their good intentions under the negativity? Pray and ask God to open your eyes and your mind to see the best in the situation.
- [ ] To identify three things regarding Jesus Christ about which you are skeptical, afraid of, or don't understand. Write them down. Pray about each item this week, that God would open your eyes to a viewpoint beyond your own.
- [ ] To "come and see" Jesus every day this week. Start in the Gospel of John, chapter 1. Spend fifteen minutes each day progressing through John, studying Jesus' life and ministry. Make note of how you view him before and after your study. What changed?

ALL WORK IS SERVICE
WEEK 50

Serve wholeheartedly, as if you were serving the Lord, not people, because you know that the Lord will reward each one for whatever good they do, whether they are slave or free.

EPHESIANS 6:7–8

I had just completed a large-scale project at work. As we closed things up, our project team sent out a post-project survey to all those touched by our work in an effort to grade our success based on the goals and metrics we had set at the beginning of the assignment.

A day later, I got a really nice e-mail from a colleague thanking our project team for our efforts.

I responded with a simple, short e-mail: "Thanks! Here to serve!"

A couple hours later I got a reply that, frankly, really startled me: "Haha well said! I know your future at (company) will not involve you serving other people."

My inner smart-aleck wanted to respond (but wisely didn't): "Well then, I guess I'll be unemployed!"

All work is service. If you aren't serving in your work, you really aren't working.

I admit I stewed and pondered over his note for quite some time before deleting it. This person is someone, in the worldly sense, I admire professionally. He has worked incredibly hard throughout his career and accomplished a great deal. He has made the organization and its customers far better. But I fear he's missing the point. So then I got to thinking. How many other people are too?

The salesperson serves customers by meeting their wants and needs. The doctor serves patients by diagnosing their pain or illness. The defense attorney serves clients by representing their case and cause. The coach serves athletes by putting them in the best possible position to be victorious. The teacher serves students by tailoring instruction to meet their individual needs. The contractor serves families by building homes to their exact specifications. The financial advisor serves retirees by creating a feasible plan to achieve their long-term goals.

Even if the salesperson, the doctor, the attorney, the coach, the teacher, the contractor, and the financial advisor are all motivated by selfish desires and self-seeking gains in their work, the lowest common denominator still holds true. At the core of their work, they are seeking to meet the needs of someone else. Even if they don't think so, they are serving. All work is service.

The words of one of my favorite communicators—Pastor Timothy Keller of Redeemer Presbyterian Church in New York City—ran through my mind:

All work, according to God's design, is service. Through work we enrich one another and become more and more interwoven. When Christians do "secular" work, they function as salt and light in the world (Matthew 5:13–16). Farming and business, childcare and law, medicine and music—all these forms of work cultivate, care for, and sustain the created world that God made and loves. We are all ministers (priests) to the human community on God's behalf. [1]

The Apostle Paul seconds this high view of our work in Ephesians chapter 6. He takes it one step further. Work isn't just service, it is serving the Lord.

"Serve wholeheartedly, as if you were serving the Lord, not people, because you know that the Lord will reward each one for whatever good they do, whether they are slave or free" (Ephesians 6:7–8).

What's fascinating about this passage is that Paul is addressing households. He starts off chapter 6 addressing children. Then in verse 4 he addresses fathers. Then he shifts gears in verse 5 in a startling way and addresses the household's slaves.

These are people who worked and served their master's every beckon, request, and call—all day, every day. All they did, all the time, was seek to meet the needs of someone else, much like the salesperson, the doctor, the attorney, the coach, the teacher, the contractor, and the financial advisor. Much like you and I.

But Paul makes a high calling even higher. Work isn't just service. It is serving the Lord. What a challenge and privilege.

This week, don't lose sight of the fact that your work—whatever it might be: raising kids, balancing budgets, treating patients, or selling products—is service to others and to God. There truly is no higher calling.

THIS WEEK, STRIVE...

☐ To make a list of all those you are serving—at work, at home, in the community, and more. Post the list where you will see it each day. What's at stake as you serve each of these people?

☐ To serve someone who is difficult for you to work with or be around. Pray and ask God to help you identify the individual. Ask him for humility and grace to approach the person with an offer to meet a need in his or her life.

☐ To assign a person to each task on your to do list as you decide what to take on this week. As you execute each endeavor, who is it that your work serves and benefits? Pray that you would serve each person well through each task—with enthusiasm and selflessness.

How Thankful?
Week 51

When you were dead in your sins and in the uncircumcision of your flesh, God made you alive with Christ. He forgave us all our sins, having canceled the charge of our legal indebtedness, which stood against us and condemned us; he has taken it away, nailing it to the cross.

COLOSSIANS 2:13–14

Do we truly understand how thankful we should be for God's saving grace?

Picture this. A family medical emergency calls you out of town suddenly for an unknown amount of time. In the mad scramble to leave town, you ask a neighbor to pick up your mail and look after the house while you are away. After being away a few weeks to support your loved ones, your bills are piling up. Another week passes and your timetable for returning home is still uncertain. The bills desperately need to be paid or they will be late, risking fees and even going to collections.

Without hesitation, your neighbor pays your bills, every last penny of them. Not one is late. Not one goes to a collection agency. He pays each one in full.

How thankful should you be? It depends on how much each bill was.

If your neighbor paid a $10 bill for a monthly magazine subscription, you will probably respond with a simple "thank you" and hand him a small wad of cash to reimburse him. But what if one of the bills that came during your absence was from the medical emergency that called you out of town? What if that bill was in excess of $250,000, far exceeding your savings?

Your neighbor paid it in full with no strings attached. How thankful should you be?

To grasp how thankful we should be for Jesus' death on the cross, we must understand the magnitude of the bill he paid.

In the aftermath of some of Jesus' greatest miracles in the city of Capernaum, a skeptical Pharisee named Simon invites Jesus to dine with him at a banquet. In that day, it was normal for the "common people" of the city to gather around the host's home and watch the "important people" having dinner at the banquet. It wouldn't be unusual for people to crowd around the exterior of the room or to stand outside the door, hoping to eavesdrop on the conversation. But one thing was forbidden—for women to talk or dine with rabbis and religious leaders in public.

During the meal, a woman boldly enters the room and approaches Jesus, sobbing. We gather from the story that she has a poor reputation in the community. Her sin bill is very large and well known. Tears flowing, she kneels and bows before him, the pouring faucet of her eyes falling to his dusty feet. She then wipes his feet clean with her hair, and pulls an expensive perfume bottle from her cloak, applying it for Jesus.

Seeing her changed heart and selfless act of love, Jesus forgives her large bill of sin. But Simon scoffs at what Jesus has done. He thinks to himself, "Only God can forgive sin. If this Jesus were really a prophet, he'd know her record and not associate with her."

But being both God and a prophet, Jesus reads Simon's mind and poses a quick scenario to the skeptical Pharisee:

"Two people owed money to a certain money lender. One owed him 500 denarii, and the other 50. Neither of them had the money to pay him back, so he forgave the debts of both. Now which of them will love him more?" (Luke 7:41–42).

The woman's bill of sin was large, and she knew it. Simon the Pharisee's sin bill was large too—pride, scoffing, harmful thoughts, judgment. But he did not know it.

Chances are, you are more often a Simon than the woman in this story. I know I am. We think we're good people who are smart and have it together. We think we're doing well on our own. But nothing is further from the truth when it comes to the sin in our lives.

How thankful you are that Jesus died for your sin is in direct proportion to your awareness of the size of your sin bill. There is no deeper sin than a sinner who doesn't know he's sinful.

But there is hope. All is not lost. We can begin to understand and appreciate the size of the bill of sin Jesus paid for us when we analyze Matthew 27:46. Jesus is hanging on the cross, dying slowly for our sin.

"About three in the afternoon Jesus cried out in a loud voice, 'Eli, Eli, lema sabachthani?' (which means 'My God, my God, why have you forsaken me?')."

The amount of the bill Jesus paid was complete separation from God. The bill was ours. It had our name and home address on it. And Jesus paid it in full.

How thankful should we be? We owe him our life. All of it.

This week, I urge you to take time to consider the astronomical cost of our bill of sin. Consider how much gratitude Jesus is due. He has "canceled the charge of our legal indebtedness, which stood against us and condemned us; he has taken it away, nailing it to the cross." Then respond in the only rational way there is: commit your life—your entire being—to him!

THIS WEEK, STRIVE...

- [ ] To consider the one person or thing for which you are most thankful in your life. I'm sure there are many things that come to mind, but pick just one. If you are able, try this exercise with another person or a small group of people.
- [ ] To take note of each response from the group. Was anyone thankful for God, for who he is, or for what his son Jesus did on the cross? How often was someone grateful for our Heavenly Father?
- [ ] To discuss with the group why God may have been an afterthought with your gratitude. Or if he was a source of gratitude for anyone in the group, why is he worthy of such praise? How can you better express your personal appreciation to your Heavenly Father?

STRATEGIC PLANNING
WEEK 52

But you will receive power when the Holy Spirit comes on you; and you will be my witnesses in Jerusalem, and in all Judea and Samaria, and to the ends of the earth.

ACTS 1:8

Every successful endeavor of which I've ever been a part had two things in common: a goal and a plan.

Goals are visionary. They are a picture of the future that produces passion. Goals excite us. They give us something to which we can look forward, place hope in, and work toward. Goals give us ideas, energy, and drive. We strive to meet our goals.

For 51 weeks this year, we've seen that God has a goal for all our aspirations, hopes and dreams—that we would come into relationship with him and use the gifts, talents, and resources he's given us to serve him in our every endeavor.

But as the old adage goes, a goal without a plan is just a wish. Plans require preparation, development, and calculation. They are tactical, take time to form, and they require hard work, critical thinking, and strategy. Plans demand execution and ownership. They are the blood, sweat, and tears of a dream.

Goals are great. But plans make it happen. So what's yours?

Fortunately, we don't have to plan alone. Jesus gave us the perfect planning template during his last moments on earth.

"But you will receive power when the Holy Spirit comes on you; and you will be my witnesses in Jerusalem, and in all Judea and Samaria, and to the ends of the earth" (Acts 1:8).

At a quick glance, this verse doesn't seem to apply well to us today. But to dismiss it without further study is a grave mistake. Containing a requirement, a role, and a roadmap, Acts 1:8 is the perfect strategic plan for a follower of Jesus Christ.

REQUIREMENT = THE HOLY SPIRIT

Simply put, to go it alone is a mistake. We cannot serve God to our fullest potential without him. He made us. He knows us best. We must let his power in us—the Holy Spirit—help us uncover who we're meant to be and what we're meant to do.

ROLE = TO BE A WITNESS

In legal terms, a witness bears testimony to true events, to what really happened. A witness has an obligation to share what he or she has seen and experienced. Christ's call to us is no different—to tell everyone what we've seen and experienced about him in our lives.

ROAD MAP = START CLOSE TO HOME

We know we need God's spirit to guide our lives. We know we are his witnesses. But where do we begin to serve? How do we execute this high calling? Jesus provides a flawless and practical plan of action to guide our way.

1. JERUSALEM

When Jesus outlined this strategic plan, he was with his disciples in Jerusalem where they were living and working in that season of ministry. God wants you to start serving where you are, in your "Jerusalem." He wants you to witness to those with whom you rub elbows every day—your friends and family; coworkers and colleagues; students, clients, and patients; at home, the gym, the office, the store. Start simple; serve where you are.

2. JUDEA

Being a witness to all Judea would've greatly broadened the geographic scope of the disciples' work. After you start impacting your Jerusalem, the next step is leaving your normal circles of activity. Break up the routine. Impact new people. You've been reading about the food bank in need in the next town over. Go do something about it. You saw the repeated stories on the news calling for donors and volunteers. What are you waiting for? Take the next step—out of the comfort of your Jerusalem and into Judea.

3. SAMARIA

Samaria was north of Jerusalem, but it might as well have been on the other side of the globe. The cultural chasm between Jews and Samaritans could not have been wider. God is calling us to reach across these cultural gaps around us. It's time to leave your cultural norms—and you don't have to leave town to do it. Maybe you need to serve the poor. Maybe you need to go meet the needs of the hungry and homeless. Maybe you need to sit and listen to the story of an addict. Maybe you need to pray with someone in grief. Remember, it's not our fault people are poor, hungry, homeless, addicted, grieving, or alone. But as Christ followers, it is our responsibility to do something about it. Will you go?

4. ENDS OF THE EARTH

When the disciples traveled by foot, animal, or boat, witnessing to "the ends of the earth" must have seemed like a daunting and impossible task! But not so for you and me. World travel is at our fingertips. Global missions, ministries, and organizations are prominent and in need of resources to operate. We really have no excuse. As we grow in our relationship with God and our service to him, we must leave our physical and cultural comfort zones to be his witnesses. Opportunities abound to serve and to give—are you willing?

Notice that no part of the roadmap is optional. God's goal for us is to know and serve him. Jesus doesn't say we must serve and witness in Jerusalem *or* Judea *or* Samaria *or* the ends of the earth. It says *and*, meaning all of the above. This is the essence of our life's journey with Christ— our level of service will naturally grow in direct proportion to the depth of our relationship with him. It's about knowing and serving.

As you close out this year and springboard into the new year to come, you have everything you need to achieve God's goal for you. If you've welcomed Jesus into your life, you have the *requirement* of the Holy Spirit. You've been given a specific *role* to fill as God's witness. You have a *roadmap* to guide you as you serve him in your Jerusalem, your Judea, your Samaria, and to the ends of the earth.

You know God's goal for you. You have your strategic plan.

Let's Strive to make it happen.

THIS WEEK, STRIVE...

- ☐ To seek God's guidance for the way in which he would have you fill your role as a witness. Is he calling you to step up your giving and generosity? Is he moving you to give of your time in service to him and others in need? Is he leading you toward a mentoring relationship with someone in whom you can invest?

- ☐ To chart the course of your local roadmap. Where is your Jerusalem? What will you accomplish there in the year ahead? Whom will you impact? How about your Judea? Where will that be? How will you exit the comfort of your normal routine to make a difference?

- ☐ To plan your roadmap for growth. Where will your Samaria be? Will it be the homeless shelter or drug rehabilitation facility across town? How will you change the lives of those whose life and background differ greatly from yours? What about the ends of the earth? Will you partner with the cause of a global missions organization? Will you travel across the country or the world to serve those in need? What is God leading you to do? Where is God leading you to go?

NOTES

Week 3 — Classroom of Pain

1. Ellen Beate Hansen Sandseter. "Categorizing risky play—how can we identify risk taking in children's play?" *European Early Childhood Education Research Journal* 15, no. 2 (2007). Retrieved from: www.tandfonline.com/doi/abs/10.1080/13502930701321733#.U wZwXChy_zI.
2. Tony Dungy, *Quiet Strength* (Carol Stream, IL: Tyndale, 2007), 181–182.
3. Timothy Keller. "The Importance of Hell." Redeemer Presbyterian Church, August 2009. Retrieved from: www.redeemer.com/redeemer-report/article/the_importance_of_hell.

Week 4 — Work

1. Sherry L. Murphy, Jiaquan Xu, and Kenneth D. Kockanek. "Deaths: Preliminary Data for 2012," *National Vital Statistics Reports,* January 11, 2010. Retrieved from: www.cdc.gov/nchs/data/nvsr/nvsr60/nvsr60_04.pdf.

Week 5 — Your Life Is Your Message

1. "Self-Described Christians Dominate America but Wrestle with Four Aspects of Spiritual Depth," *Barna Group,* September 13, 2011. Retrieved from: www.barna.org/barna-update/faith-spirituality/524-self-described-christians-dominate-america-but-wrestle-with-four-aspects-of-spiritual-depth#.VG_NJPnF-So.

Week 10 — Waiting Rooms

1. Jeff Manion, *The Land Between: Finding God in Difficult Transitions.* (Grand Rapids, MI: Zondervan, 2010), 36–126.

WEEK 16—TOO MUCH

1. "Last year's drought was good for grapes, winemakers say," *CBC News*, April 14, 2013. Retrieved from: www.cbc.ca/news/canada/ottawa/ last-year-s-drought-was-good-for-grapes-winemakers-say-1.1341392.

WEEK 18—THE CANCER OF ENTITLEMENT

1. Tim Elmore, "From Entitled to Empowered: Building Four Virtues in Students to Combat Entitlement in the Classroom, *Huffington Post*. February 19, 2014. Retrieved from: www.huffingtonpost.com/tim-elmore/from-entitled-to-empowere_b_4804516.html.
2. Michael Lewis, "Don't Eat Fortune's Cookie." *News at Princeton*, June 3, 2012. Retrieved from: www.princeton.edu/main/news/archive/S33/87/54K53/index.xml?section=.

WEEK 21—HUMBITION

1. Dan Schwabel, "Millennials vs. Baby Boomers: Who Would You Rather Hire?" *Time Business & Money*. March 29, 2012. Retrieved from: http://business.time.com/2012/03/29/millennials-vs-baby-boomers-who-would-you-rather-hire/.

WEEK 24—UNLESS

1. "You Lost Me: Why Young Christians are Leaving Church . . . and Rethinking Faith." *Barna Group*, November 16, 2011. Retrieved from: www.barna.org/teens-next-gen-articles/534-five-myths-about-young-adult-church-dropouts.
2. Dr. Seuss, *The Lorax*. (New York: Random House, 1971).

WEEK 30—FAMILY MATTERS?

1. Rachel M. Shattuck and Rose M. Kreider, "Social and Economic Characteristics of Currently Unmarried Women With a Recent

Birth: 2011," *US Census Bureau,* May 2013. Retrieved from: www.census.gov/prod/2013pubs/acs-21.pdf.

WEEK 33—THE EXCHANGE

Sam Borden, "For U.S. Relayers, Dread of Another Dropped Baton," *New York Times.* July 23, 2012. Retrieved from: www.nytimes.com/2012/07/23/sports/olympics/olympics-2012-us-track-relays-hope-to-avoid-another-baton-drop.html?pagewanted=all&_r=2&.

WEEK 36—THE RESPONSIBILITY OF FREEDOM

1. Tim Elmore, "What Does Freedom Require?" *Growing Leaders.* N.p., July 4, 2013. Retrieved from: http://growingleaders.com/blog/what-does-freedom-require/.

WEEK 39—KEEP YOUR TESTS TESTS

1. "Behind The Enron Scandal," *Time,* n.d. Retrieved from: http://content.time.com/time/specials/packages/0,28757,2021097,00.html.
2. "SEC Enforcement Actions: Insider Trading Cases," *US Securities and Exchange Commission,* October 25, 2013. Retrieved from: www.sec.gov/spotlight/insidertrading/cases.shtml.

WEEK 48—WASTING TIME

1. "American Time Use Study," *US Department of Labor,* October 23, 2013. Retrieved from: www.bls.gov/tus/charts/.
2. "Zero-TV Doesn't Mean Zero Video," *Nielsen,* March 11, 2013. Retrieved from: www.nielsen.com/us/en/newswire/2013/zero-tv-doesnt-mean-zero-video.html.

WEEK 50—ALL WORK IS SERVICE

1. Timothy Keller, "Vocation: Discerning Your Calling." *Redeemer City to City.* (New York: Redeemer Presbyterian Church, 2007). Retrieved from: http://cdn.theresurgence.com/files/2011/06/06/Vocation-Discerning_Your_Calling.pdf?1307425464.

ABOUT THE AUTHOR

It would be hard to find many men more respected for the combination of faith, leadership, and character than Tim Hiller.

Hailing from Orrville, Ohio, Hiller re-wrote the record books as a quarterback at Western Michigan University from 2005-09, while maintaining a 4.0 GPA, and earning his undergraduate and graduate degrees. While at WMU, Hiller co-founded the school's Fellowship of Christian Athletes huddle and was winner of the 2009 Wuerffel Trophy, honoring academic, athletic, and community service endeavors. Hiller was also an Academic All-American and a finalist for the William V. Campbell Trophy honoring the National Scholar Athlete of the Year.

After his collegiate career, Hiller spent one year in the NFL, primarily with the Indianapolis Colts. He is a frequently requested speaker across the Midwest and has coached high school football each year since his playing career ended, including three years as the Head Football Coach at Gull Lake High School in Richland, Michigan.

Hiller and his wife, Michelle, and son Daniel reside in Kalamazoo, Michigan, where he is employed by Stryker Corporation and is co-owner of Next Level Performance, LLC, which delivers sport-specific training to athletes with a primary focus on leadership and character development.

To get to know Tim more or to request him as a speaker, please visit:

www.timhiller.com

or follow him on Facebook and Twitter (@timhiller3).

To learn more about Next Level Performance, please visit:

www.nlathlete.com